10

Falcons Return

JOHN KAUFMANN
AND HEINZ MENG

Falcons Return

illustrated with 106 photographs

WILLIAM MORROW AND COMPANY
New York   1975

BY THE SAME AUTHOR

Birds in Flight
Chimney Swift
Fish Hawk
Flying Hand-Launched Gliders
Insect Travelers
Winds and Weather
Wings, Sun, and Stars

ACKNOWLEDGMENTS

The authors wish to thank the following people and organizations for their valuable assistance: David G. Allen, Dr. Dean Amadon, G. Ronald Austing, James Baird, Don Bleitz, Dr. Tom Cade, Robert L. Coffin, Phyllis Dague, Yvon Desautels, Dr. James Enderson, Mrs. Robert Jevon, George Laycock, R. Wayne Nelson, Charles A. Proctor, Carol Taylor, Hobart M. Van Deusen, Aletta Vett, James Weaver, Ted Williams; Cornell University Laboratory of Ornithology, Dartmouth College, Massachusetts Audubon Society, Massachusetts Division of Fisheries and Game, Smithsonian Institution Archives, State University of New York College at New Paltz, Sun Life Assurance Company of Canada.

CONTENTS

For Peter Paul Meng and Adam Minassian

PART I

The Peregrine

*I*t is a clear day with a light breeze blowing. A car pulls up beside a dirt road running through farm country. The driver gets out, slings a big canvas bag over his shoulder, and puts on a heavy leather glove. He reaches into the rear of the car.

Perched on a padded bar, a peregrine falcon waits under the darkness of her hood. The falconer coaxes her onto his glove, grasps the leather straps, or jesses, fastened to her legs, and lifts her out of the car. The hooded bird rouses, half opening her wings as the falconer makes a few adjustments. Then he slips off the hood. Her dark, piercing eyes flash in the light as he releases her. Her strong, sharp wings dig into the air, and she rapidly picks up speed. Beating fast, she climbs in a swift, high spiral. Far above the field, she levels off and circles easily with her wings and tail spread wide, riding the warm, rising currents of air.

The falconer pulls a fluttering pigeon from his bag. He tosses the pigeon into the air and shouts to the falcon, "Ho!" Dashing straight and flat, the pigeon flies toward the cover of some trees at the edge of the field. High overhead the watching falcon slides off to one side, folds her wings, and dives. Faster and faster she streaks down toward the pigeon, then her sharp-taloned feet shoot out and hit it with a sound like a punching fist. Feathers

7

Left: Falconer preparing to release his peregrine. *John Kaufmann*

Above: Peregrine hunting.
G. Ronald Austing

fly out, and the pigeon falls to the ground. The falcon circles down and lands on it with her wings spread wide. She jabs her beak down and cuts through the neck and spinal cord of the stunned pigeon to finish her kill. The falconer moves in slowly and gently picks up the peregrine and her prey. He grasps her jesses once again and lets her feed on the pigeon.

The peregrine: what sort of bird is it in nature, apart from hood, glove, and man? First, it is a bird of prey, a raptor, and one member of a larger family, the falcons. In scientific terms, within the order Falconiformes, day-flying birds of prey, peregrines and other falcons belong to the family Falconidae and the genus *Falco*. The peregrine's species designation is *Falco peregrinus*.

Falcons have large, powerful eyes and small, compact heads, often marked with dark moustache stripes. Their bodies are highly streamlined and tightly feathered, and their wings are long and stiffly pointed for fast flight. Falcons are primarily open country birds, built for long speed chases and steeply plunging dives, or stoops. Their large strong feet and sharp, deeply curved

Peregrine back on the glove after downing a pigeon.   *John Kaufmann*

talons are designed to strike their quarry a devastating blow in midair. Their beaks are notched to sever the spinal cord of their prey and sharply hooked to tear off meat.

Gyrfalcons are the largest falcons, followed by the peregrines, then by the much smaller merlins and the kestrels. Probably the peregrine is the most superb all-around aerial hunter of this remarkable family. Its great speed, over 200 miles per hour in the dive, its good maneuverability, and formidable striking power enable it to take a greater variety of winged prey than the other falcons. Its graceful soaring commands the skies, and its awesome diving, falling like a feathered bomb to explode upon its prey, is a spectacular and chilling sight. This mastery of flight and deadly hunting skill have always made the peregrine one of the most exciting and admired of all birds.

In North America there are three subspecies of the peregrine. The arctic, or tundra peregrine, *Falco peregrinus tundrius,* ranges across the tundra of Alaska and Canada to the coasts of Greenland. The Peale's peregrine, *Falco peregrinus pealei,* inhabits the area from the Aleutian Islands of Alaska down through the Queen Charlotte Islands of British Columbia. The American peregrine, *Falco peregrinus anatum,* which formerly inhabited much of the eastern half of the United States, some areas as far west as California, and many parts of Canada, now has a much reduced range. By the early 1960's it had completely disappeared from the eastern United States, had almost vanished in the West, and sharply dropped in numbers in Canada. A close relative of the peregrine, the prairie falcon, *Falco mexicanus,* still survives west of the Mississippi, but in numbers far fewer than before.

Among the larger species of falcons, the females are about one third larger and heavier than the males. Their greater size, weight, and strength enable them to strike down larger prey. For this reason falconers of old preferred them to the males and

Immature female (left) and male peregrines, showing difference in size.
Heinz Meng

called only the female *falcon*. The male was called *tiercel,* the word coming originally from the Latin *tertius,* meaning "third," because of the one third difference in size and weight.

There are probably several reasons why the female peregrine is larger. Her greater size, weight, and strength may help her to dominate the male during nesting, when their lives center around her activities with the eggs and young. However, there is another more important reason. The smaller, lighter male is more adept at chasing and outmaneuvering small- and medium-sized birds. He is the chief provider during the nesting period, bringing food for the female to feed to the young. In any peregrine habitat there are many more small- and medium-sized birds than large birds. If the male was as large as his mate, he could not exploit this greater abundance of smaller prey as fully. He could not provide as steady a supply of food if he had to hunt larger birds, simply because there are fewer of them. So the male peregrine's size and thus his hunting ability help furnish a constant, reliable food supply for the peregrine family during a critical period.

11

Peregrine cliffs at Millbrook Mountain on the Shawangunk Ridge near New Paltz, New York, and close-up showing cliff ledges. *John Kaufmann*

The peregrine's year begins in late February or early March, when the males return from their winter in the South to re-occupy their nesting cliffs. The females usually arrive from one to three weeks later, although some pairs spend the winter together and reach their cliff at the same time. Peregrines mate for life. When one partner dies, the survivor takes a new mate. If one pair fails to return to their cliff, a new pair will take it over.

12

Thus, although the individual birds may change, the same cliffs are used year after year.

The cliff is usually a steep, sometimes vertical rock face, and the peregrine's nesting place, or eyrie, is usually located on a narrow ledge on the upper part of the face. The eyrie normally overlooks a valley, river, lake, or seacoast. However, eyries have

View from an eyrie overlooking the Connecticut River Valley at Fairlee Cliffs, Vermont, in the 1930's. *Hobart M. Van Deusen*

also been found in such seemingly unlikely places as the high ledges of city skyscrapers. Wherever it is, the eyrie commands a wide view of the sky and a panorama below, across which the peregrines can spot, pursue, and strike in the open, when the prey is too far from cover to escape their swift dash and lightning stoop.

The peregrine cliff at Mount Tom, Massachusetts, 1928. The eyrie is on the ledge at the lower center of the photograph.   *Robert L. Coffin*

A tiercel on his favorite perch by the cliff.

Joseph A. Hagar and Robert L. Coffin

After reclaiming his cliff, the tiercel guards it against intruders, especially others of his species. Peregrines defend the sky all around the cliff and will vigorously attack any threatening bird coming within a radius of about 500 feet of the eyrie and will drive off others at much greater distances. Peregrines hunt far and wide; some of their hunting territories measure up to twenty square miles. Accordingly, the eyries are not usually found less than two miles apart. Under exceptional conditions, however, they may be much closer together, as on northern sea cliffs where huge colonies of birds nest, when prey is close by and extremely abundant.

Awaiting his falcon in spring, the tiercel perches on a dead tree jutting out from the cliff. He cocks his head to one side then the other, directing his gaze upward. Far below, flickers, robins, meadowlarks, blue jays, and other birds are flying back and forth. But the tiercel is not watching them. Suddenly his head stops moving, and his eye fixes on a distant point high in the sky.

Invisible to the human eye, the falcon races closer on the brisk south wind. The birds below dive for cover as her familiar shape sails overhead, the sharply bent wings propelling the streamlined body at great speed. The tiercel launches out from the tree and starts flying back and forth along the cliff face, calling repeatedly a pleading "weechew, weechew!" He alights on

Falcon descending.   *John Kaufmann*

one ledge for an instant, calls, and takes off to land on another, crouches low and calls again and again to tempt her with the nesting places on his cliff.

The falcon sees the cliff below and hears the coaxing cries of the tiercel, fluttering his display. She circles several times on high, watching and listening. Then she drives forward and down with several quick beats and folds her wings. Moments later, after a thousand-foot plunge, she zooms upward in front of the cliff and lands softly near the tiercel. The cliff has drawn them together again.

At the start of courtship the tiercel is very active and leads the falcon on. Feeding is part of the ritual that arouses them toward mating. After daybreak they watch for passing prey. The tiercel may dart out to intercept a flicker or blue jay flapping along through the early mist. Or he may set out on a long reconnaissance flight across the valley. Today his first kill is a blue jay. Hurtling down from on high, he snap rolls at the last instant after the wildly twisting jay, which almost eludes his final split-second grab. The jay's life ebbs in a second, and it hangs limp in the tiercel's grip.

"Weechew! Weechew!" he calls, as he wings back toward the cliff and the tree where the falcon waits. She calls in return and flies out to meet him. The two converge rapidly until the tiercel pulls up steeply and releases the jay as the falcon rolls upside down below him to catch the tumbling bird in her outthrust talons. At other times she may take the prey directly from his grasp. Then he escorts her back to the tree. Again and again as mating time draws near, he brings food and passes it to her.

Sometimes the pair may set out to hunt together. If so, she makes the first stoop. If she misses, he may follow her in to take the bird on the second pass. She always eats the first kill, whether

17

she makes it herself or he presents it to her. Sometimes the tiercel lands beside her on a branch with food. Bowing slowly up and down, turning his head completely over and chittering softly, he passes it to her. At about this time, while the tiercel still hunts far and wide, the falcon begins to stay closer to the cliff.

During the courtship days of March, the tiercel displays his flying skill and bravado to impress and arouse his mate. Sometimes she flies out with him, and they call loudly back and forth as they dive toward one another, pull up, and touch in midair. But most often she watches from the tree and follows his aerial gyrations with her shining, deep-brown eyes. He spreads his wings and tail wide and rides buoyantly aloft on strong thermal currents flowing upward from the sunbaked rocks. He spirals up and disappears into the clear sky overhead. Suddenly he re-appears with wings furled, falling like a streamlined stone. At full speed along the cliff face he begins to open his wings, then pulls up, up, upside down, then down, up, and over as he loops again and again with the air whining through his wing-tip feathers.

When the wind blows strongly, the tiercel's flight becomes even more daring. Blasting up and over the cliff, the high winds are like a surging sea whose waves and troughs he exploits. He dives right at the cliff face, heading into the wind. At the final instant before crashing, he rolls tightly and zooms upward, bounding higher and higher within the shallow layer of air running close over the peak. Inches from the rock, he rips past the falcon with a roaring *whoosh*. Now the full blast hits him and lifts him high overhead like an elevator. He zigzags up and down in a sawtooth pattern, then plunges again to loop, roll, and dart along in front of the sharp crags. With many variations and endless daring he conquers the wind, the cliff, and the watching eye of the falcon.

18

Tiercel.   *John Kaufmann*

As March draws on, the tiercel continues his showy flights, but now he begins to court the falcon in a different way. He flies to several ledges that he has picked as possible nesting spots. He spends a lot of time scratching around on the ledges and facing outward, wailing "weechew, weechew" in a strange low tone. He flies to the falcon and perches with her, calling all the time. At first she seems to ignore him completely, but then the mating urge becomes all-powerful, and the ritual takes effect. She flies to a ledge while he is scratching there, and the pair call rapidly and loudly together. She flies back to the tree. He calls from the ledge in great excitement, flies from the cliff to the tree, and balances himself atop her with flapping wings as their high-pitched chittering cries fill the air. During the following days they come together many times on the tree, cliff top, or ledges to mate.

Now the falcon spends more time on the cliff ledges, while the tiercel loses interest in them. When he is off hunting, she inspects the various ledges and chooses one, usually between twenty-five to fifty feet down from the top of the cliff. She prepares the nesting spot, or scrape, by simply scratching with her

19

claws and rubbing around with her body to form a bare hollow an inch or two deep in the dirt, rock chips, twigs, and grasses that cover the ledge. Falcons, unlike most other birds of prey, do not construct nests.

Soon the falcon starts to lay her eggs. Peregrine eggs are somewhat smaller and rounder than chicken eggs, with reddish brown markings richly mottled over an off-white or light tan background. The clutch, the total number of eggs she lays, consists of three or four, sometimes five, or very rarely six. They are

A clutch of eggs in the scrape at Mount Tom, Massachusetts, 1928.
Robert L. Coffin

Tiercel incubating the eggs at Holt's Ledge, near Hanover, New Hampshire, 1931.   *Charles A. Proctor*

laid at one- or two-day intervals. She begins incubating, or brooding, the eggs, warming them with her body, after laying the second or third egg. The falcon does most of the incubating herself during the first two weeks and only leaves the eggs to take food from her mate, to bathe, or to hunt for brief periods. When she leaves, the tiercel takes her place warming the eggs. After two weeks she hunts more and he incubates more than before.

The eggs hatch between thirty-two to thirty-five days after incubation begins. The chicks emerge from the shells covered with a short coat of white down. Their eyes are open. Their leg muscles are weak, so they cannot stand. But their gaping mouths and high, shrill voices work very well, and they cry out for food.

At first the falcon stays close to the young chicks, brooding them while the tiercel does most of the hunting. When he brings a bird, she flies off the scrape to receive it at a regularly used

21

Above: Peregrine with young chick and two eggs ready to hatch, at a California eyrie.   *Don Bleitz*

Opposite: Tiercel, just landed at the eyrie with prey he has killed and partly eaten.   *Joseph A. Hagar and Robert L. Coffin*

Below: Falcon brooding her chicks at Holt's Ledge, near Hanover, New Hampshire, 1931.   *Charles A. Proctor*

plucking block on the limb or stump of a dead tree. She first severs the neck, then plucks, or plumes, the bird to remove most of the feathers, which are indigestible. She then carries the prey to the scrape, strips off small pieces of meat, and feeds the chicks. In addition, she also bites off small pieces of breastbone for her young. This food provides calcium for their growing bones and prevents rickets.

Since the chicks cannot stand or move about at first, they keep their places when they are fed. The falcon feeds the most demanding chick first. It is usually the oldest and largest, but because hunger makes the younger and smaller ones very active in demanding food, they too get their share. At first the feeding is fairly orderly, but as they grow quickly the young become more lively and aggressive when food is brought in. Then the

Falcon feeding her young, almost three weeks old, Holt's Ledge, near Hanover, New Hampshire, 1931.   *Charles A. Proctor*

falcon must work fast to keep up with their appetites, tearing off a dozen or more pieces each minute for them to gulp down. When a chick is full, its crop, the food storage pouch in its throat, bulges out. The crop acts as a holding chamber until the stomach is ready to take in more food and digest it.

By about three weeks of age the peregrine nestlings are much bigger and stronger and they scramble and fight to take food. After about four weeks the falcon parents just drop the prey near the scrape for the young to tear apart themselves. Now the older, larger, and stronger ones have a real advantage. Older females, already bigger and stronger than the males, can command the most food. Older, stronger males have an upper hand over younger males in the feeding free-for-alls that erupt when food arrives.

Peregrine chicks, almost three weeks old, with full crops after feeding. Holt's Ledge, near Hanover, New Hampshire, 1931.   *Charles A. Proctor*

There is a wild melee of thrashing wings, clawing, and screaming as they struggle to grab the prey. Usually the first one to get
a firm grip drags the prey beneath its body and partly spreads
its wings and tail to cover and keep it away from the others as
it feeds. Weak or defective nestlings cannot survive this first real
competition for food. Probably between 30 to 50 percent of
young peregrines die before the time has come to leave the nest.

If a predator should attack the eyrie, the young birds fall on
their backs screeching, with their claws thrust toward the attacker. However, peregrines are not bothered by most predators.

Peregrine nestling, a little more than four weeks old. Holt's Ledge, near
Hanover, New Hampshire, 1931.   *Charles A. Proctor*

Falcon defending her eyrie on a skyscraper ledge.
G. Harper Hall—courtesy of Massachusetts Audubon Society

The eyries are usually inaccessible to raccoons, snakes, foxes, and other ground predators that devour bird eggs and chicks. Then, too, ravens, crows, gulls, jaegers, certain hawks, owls, and other nest-robbing birds usually avoid the lair of a killer that can appear out of nowhere, hurtling at terrific speed to strike a swift, deadly blow. Peregrines drive off eagles and large hawks. They have split the skull of red-shouldered hawks that ventured too close to the eyrie. A large snowy owl that killed a peregrine chick and flew off with it was knocked out of the sky like a pigeon by the tremendous slashing strike of the avenging parent. The terrific impact of its stoop, with gravity seeming to add a ton to every ounce, makes the peregrine and its eyrie something for any knowing predator to avoid.

27

Falcon confronting camera as she touches down on the eyrie ledge.
Joseph A. Hagar and Robert L. Coffin

Man, however, is harder to discourage. To rob a clutch of handsome eggs, to steal a nestling, to photograph the eyrie or band the young, men have gone down to the ledges on ropes. Usually the screaming parents have made close, swooping passes without striking. However, some birds, desperately defending their young, have gashed the scalps and shoulders of those disturbing the eyrie. Yet ultimately man is the only intruder or predator against which the peregrine has no defense.

Despite their reputation as deadly hunters, peregrines are driven away from nesting territories where they do not belong by much smaller birds. Both the darting kingbird and the agile sharp-shinned hawk can easily outmaneuver the straight-flying, wide-turning hunter of the open country. If the peregrine should try to counterattack, only a lucky swipe of its claws in passing will stop the smaller bird from defending its territory.

On the other hand, birds such as the phoebe that the peregrine normally preys upon may nest very close to an eyrie without being disturbed. Like most other birds of prey, the peregrine rarely hunts in the immediate vicinity of its home. The close-nesting birds thus not only minimize the threat from their normal

28

predator, but also enjoy the protection of the eyrie area provided by their "hosts."

There is one danger the young peregrines constantly face until they can fly, that of falling from the ledge. A narrow shelf on a high rocky cliff is a precarious perch. When the young ones are small, they do not move about much, so they are safe. But when they grow larger and stronger and start their battling tugs-of-war over food, the ledge becomes a dangerous place. Nestlings have been seen tumbling off, hurtling down, and smashing on the rocks below.

The danger of the cliff becomes even more real when the young peregrines are almost ready to fly. They develop their wing muscles by jumping up into the air a foot or two and flapping hard for a few moments before sinking back down to the

Two nestlings about four weeks old, the one in the rear exercising its still-developing wings. Holt's Ledge, near Hanover, New Hampshire, 1931.

Charles A. Proctor

ledge. One mistake, such as leaping too high in a strong wind, or flapping out a couple of feet beyond the ledge, can send an unready, overeager young bird swiftly down to death.

The parent peregrine links its flight to food and hunting even before the nestling first leaves the ledge where it was hatched. The falcon approaches carrying a bird. The young ones scream frantically and jump about. But the falcon does not drop off the food. Instead she sails past, displaying it to the young, tempting them to fly out after it. When one is ready, it will fly out and try to snatch the prey from her talons. Another tactic the parents use to lure their young into the air is simply to bring no food at all and force them to fly if they want to eat. The sight of their parents holding food on the plucking block near the eyrie is enough to get the young birds to try their wings.

From the time it hatches until it is ready to fly, a young pere-grine's plumage changes from a mere thin coating of down

Young peregrines at about five weeks, almost ready to fly. Holt's Ledge, near Hanover, New Hampshire, 1931. *Charles A. Proctor*

into the precisely structured feathering of a bird magnificently equipped for flight. At two weeks a thicker, furlike coating of down insulates the chick, which is no longer brooded by its parents. At three weeks the first feathers poke out through the down. At five weeks, although still patched here and there with down, the peregrine is fully feathered in its first, or juvenal, plumage. Its upper surfaces, the streakings on its light gray breast, and its moustache marks are all a rich, dark brown. The undersurfaces of its wings are heavily marked, or barred, and its tail is marked underneath with light crossbars on a dark background.

When they are between five and six weeks old, the young peregrines take to the air. The first ones to leave the ledge wait at other spots on or near the cliff and fly out to take food when their parents bring it. Finally, the last one remains at the eyrie, standing alone on the brink of empty space, looking out into the

Last of the young ready to leave the eyrie. Holt's Ledge, near Hanover, New Hampshire, 1931.   *Charles A. Proctor*

Young peregrine taking off. *John Kaufmann*

vast sea of air before it and the countryside spread out far
below. The wind ruffles its feathers. It has faced the wind,
flapped its wings, and hesitated many times, but now it launches
itself forward and out into the air. It has never flown, but it
immediately responds to the forces of air and gravity and begins
the complex, coordinated movements of flight. Perhaps it circles
out and down to the same dead tree where it has seen its parents
perch. Then, beating its wings back and forth, spreading its tail
to brake its speed, the young bird lands awkwardly but safely.

Every day the fledgling peregrines become more skillful fliers.
They fly out with their parents to watch and learn the techniques
of hunting birds in the air. The falcon and tiercel catch birds,
soar above their screeching offspring, and drop the prey. The
young peregrines beat toward the dead bird tumbling down
through the air, and one of them snatches it. They practice again
and again and so sharpen their timing and coordination for the
attack. By pursuing birds and imitating their parents they learn
how to stoop from on high, to close in from above, to the side of,

John Kaufmann

or underneath their prey, to swing over upside down and kick their feet at the moment of impact for added killing power. Smaller birds often die instantly from the force of the blow and the crushing grasp of the big feet and sickle-shaped talons. Larger birds do not always die at once, but they do not suffer long. Young peregrines instinctively use their powerful, notched beak, seize the neck of their downed prey, and cut through the spinal cord quickly to kill any bird that survives the aerial assault. This behavior is an automatic action, which is even used on prey that has been killed in flight. It probably originated in the peregrine's need to protect its eyes from the beaks of birds that were still alive.

If they succeed in making the kill, the young peregrines have their meal. However, if they are unable to catch their prey at first, the parents are there to provide them with food after prolonged, loud screaming. Indeed, the adults themselves do not always succeed in the attack—a good percentage of birds seem to escape them. But one thing must be kept in mind. Young peregrines are not the only ones that practice hunting. The adults do so too in order to keep their flight and attack very sharp. Like great human athletes and performers, their superb skill requires constant practice. Peregrines have often been seen "playing," harassing other birds by stooping at them without striking, perhaps just tapping them with a closed foot, or scattering a flock of birds without pursuing any single member. Because of this practicing and the fact that the seriousness of their attack depends on how hungry they are, an observer cannot judge the effectiveness of wild peregrines accurately by counting how many kills they make out of a certain number of attempts.

After a couple of months the young peregrines become sufficiently adept at hunting to care for themselves. Their family bond loosens, so by the time they move south in autumn each young bird is on its own, an independent traveler. After their first year, the juvenile feathers start to molt, gradually falling out and being replaced by their adult plumage. Their brown upper parts become slate gray. Their caps darken, and their face marks blacken. Their breast color lightens to off-white or rich buff marked with elegant dark accents. Under their wings the barred pattern also lightens, and the undersides of their tail feathers become light with dark crossbars. Before long they will look just like their parents, and in several years when they mature they too will come north to raise their young in cliffside eyries.

Today, however, with some very rare exceptions in the western regions, peregrines no longer live and breed in the United States. Their downfall began in the late 1940's, when something strange and terrible took place at peregrine eyries throughout the country. The cliffs, which for countless springtimes had echoed the high, sharp calls of falcons and tiercels, fell silent. At Mount

Tom, Mount Everett, and Rattlesnake Mountain in Massachusetts, Holt's Ledge near Hanover, New Hampshire, Taughannock Falls near Ithaca, New York, Englewood Cliffs in New Jersey, Nockamixon Cliffs in Pennsylvania, Black Mountain in North Carolina, from Maine to Wisconsin to Missouri to California, the peregrines were dying off.

By the early 1960's a number of scientists strongly suspected that long-term pesticides, which had first come into wide use in 1946, were responsible for sharp declines in the populations of ospreys, bald eagles, a number of other birds, and finally peregrines. Before many years had passed, these suspicions were sadly confirmed. Predators like the peregrine exist at the peak of a food-chain pyramid. In the peregrine's case, when crops are sprayed, insects eating the plants concentrate the pesticide residues in their body tissues. Birds eat these insects, further concentrating the poisons in their own bodies. Then peregrines eat the birds, absorbing and multiplying the already highly concentrated doses. Peregrines eat a high percentage of pesticide-laden birds, because they are handicapped and cannot escape attack as well as normal individuals. Normally their tendency to attack the easiest quarry available serves to eliminate sick, feeble, or otherwise inferior birds from the breeding stock of their prey species and improves the prey population as a whole. However, when pesticides are the cause of the prey birds' enfeeblement, the whole design of nature is shattered, and the pathways of poison converge upon the peregrine.

Birds that absorb lethal doses of pesticides are a pitiful sight. They go into seizures, trembling, thrashing wildly, and foaming at the mouth as the poisons destroy their nervous systems. However, most pesticide poisoning is much more subtle and insidious, with almost no outward sign except that at nesting time no young birds are to be seen. The whole complex and marvelous

35

process of creating new life is attacked silently and incessantly from within by sublethal amounts of pesticide residues. For years no one knew or could prove this process, and very few even suspected it. Because almost no one fully realized how pervasive and catastrophic a threat pesticides were, the alarm was not sounded until it was too late to save the peregrines in most of the United States.

In the peregrine's case, there were several good reasons for the lack of awareness. In the best of times peregrines were never found in great abundance; one estimate sets the peak breeding population of the United States outside Alaska at 1,000 pairs. The limited number of suitable nesting cliffs, the fact that usually only one breeding pair occupied even the largest cliff, and the wide hunting territory required by each pair always held down their numbers.

At the time the numbers of peregrine young started to decline sharply, few people were closely watching the nesting pairs. For various reasons there was a sharply reduced surveillance of the eyries by expert observers just after World War II, at the exact time that pesticides began to be used. Then, too, bird watchers generally tended to ignore peregrines, which were not usually found near large cities with active bird clubs that kept track of nesting species. To watch peregrines, an observer had to seek them out; to study them seriously he had to be dedicated. Misleading, too, was the fact that peregrines were still seen around their old haunts, although they were no longer mating or raising young. They were remnants of the past, great masters of the sky now living a kind of hollow half-life, unable to perpetuate their kind. During the autumn migration south along the Atlantic coast, peregrines from northern and eastern Canada, from Labrador and Greenland, still largely unaffected by pesticides, were seen in the same numbers as before. This evidence probably led both bird watchers who saw them and falconers who trapped them into believing that the problem of decreasing numbers in the old eyries of the United States was less important and perhaps even temporary.

Even when the direct evidence of nest failure was seen by an expert observer at the eyrie, the real cause could not be determined. Joseph Hagar was the chief hawk warden of the Massachusetts Division of Fisheries and Game during the 1930's, a time of intense interest in peregrines, when fourteen eyries in that state were carefully watched and protected against egg collectors,

Warning sign left at eyrie protected by the Massachusetts Division of Fisheries and Game in the 1930's. Peregrines were traditionally called "duck hawks." *Joseph A. Hagar and Robert L. Coffin*

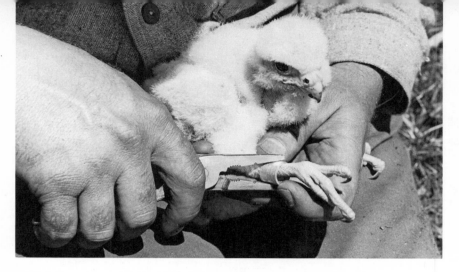

Peregrine chick being banded in Massachusetts during the 1930's.
Joseph A. Hagar and Robert L. Coffin

gunners, and some underhanded falconers who stole the nestlings even though taking them had been declared illegal. Hagar's careful and eloquent descriptions of the peregrines he observed at that time still make up a large part of what we know about their life habits.

In 1946, a spot check of the Massachusetts eyries showed that peregrines were producing even more young than before the war, probably because egg collecting as a hobby had largely died out. Hagar set up a blind at an eyrie on the cliffs of Prescott Peninsula overlooking the quiet waters of Quabbin Reservoir in the central part of the state. He and a photographer friend, Robert Coffin, took a series of pictures of the nesting birds.

In 1946, the pair produced five eggs and four fledglings. In 1947, the falcon laid three eggs, and all seemed well until one day Hagar discovered that two of the eggs were broken. Broken eggs in peregrine scrapes were a rare occurrence. The parents abandoned the scrape and recycled, starting their courtship and mating again. This time the falcon laid four eggs, but only one hatched, and the chick soon died. The next year, 1948, the same pair produced a total of five eggs in two clutches, none of which

38

Above, top: Falcon brooding her young at Quabbin Reservoir, Massachusetts, in 1946.   *Joseph A. Hagar and Robert L. Coffin*

Above: Falcon standing over her young brood at Quabbin Reservoir, Massachusetts, 1946.   *Joseph A. Hagar and Robert L. Coffin*

hatched. In 1949, their single egg also failed to hatch. In 1950, from a total of five eggs, four broke and the fifth disappeared. Then in the spring of 1951 the pair came back to the cliff but

39

did not mate. Afterward Hagar never saw them again. Indeed, after 1951 no one in Massachusetts saw any nesting peregrines; that was the year they disappeared.

Since he was only watching the one eyrie (surveillance of the others had been stopped for lack of funds), Hagar did not realize that peregrines at all the other eyries were also in grave trouble. He was deeply puzzled, but since he had seen raccoon tracks at the eyrie, he believed that these known nest robbers had been destroying the eggs and young. With hindsight his mistake is apparent. But at that time, when nothing was known about their hidden effects on wildlife, Hagar and others did not suspect that pesticides were the cause of these nesting failures. Years later, when the truth became known, Hagar sadly realized that in 1946 he had seen and photographed the last known successful nesting of peregrines in his state, and that in 1947 he had been the first to observe the strange and deadly effect of pesticides in the eyrie at Quabbin Reservoir.

In the late 1950's in England, Dr. David Ratcliffe, of the Nature Conservancy, had been receiving very strange reports of broken eggs found in peregrine scrapes throughout the British Isles. Pondering the sharp decline of peregrines and other birds of prey in Britain, Ratcliffe decided that only an extraordinary and widespread change in the whole environment could have been the cause. Thinking along these lines, he found only one recent change in the whole ecological system drastic enough to have almost wiped out entire populations of predatory birds. This change was the sudden and widespread use in Great Britain of chlorinated hydrocarbon pesticides, most notably DDT, for agricultural and other insect control work starting about 1955.

When Ratcliffe chemically analyzed the addled or infertile eggs of peregrines, he found the residues of four pesticides, including large amounts of DDE, which was later discovered to be formed during the breakdown process of DDT within the bird's body. At first he believed that the nerve poisons in pesticides might have caused deranged and destructive behavior among adult peregrines, such as failure to incubate. Earlier Ratcliffe himself had observed an incubating falcon eating one of her own eggs. However, he kept his mind open to other possibilities.

One day, while handling a broken peregrine eggshell, he noticed how thin and light it felt. He weighed it and other shells from different eyries and checked their wall thickness. Then he had the inspired idea of comparing the recent shells with those that had been collected from eyries before pesticides were first used in England.

For many years British egg collectors, probably the world's most fanatical, had been systematically robbing whole clutches from eyries, meticulously recording the date, place, and other information, blowing out the shells, and carefully preserving them in prized collections. Since peregrine eggs were considered among the most handsome, there was a plentiful supply.

Ratcliffe found that shell weights since 1946 had dropped almost 19 percent, with the sharpest decrease since 1955, when pesticides came into wide use in Great Britain. Because the eggs were still the same size as earlier ones, the later shells were considerably thinner and weaker. Peregrines lay their eggs directly on rock ledges, with little or no material to cushion them from hard shocks. They are notoriously rough on their eggs, often stepping or jumping on them or even kicking them accidentally while moving about the eyrie. Normally the shells are strong enough to stand a lot of this abuse, but the thinned-down shells were not—they would even break under nothing more than the weight of the incubating parent. Thus, Ratcliffe's first idea, that pesticide-dosed peregrines had shown abnormal behavior and eaten their intact eggs, now appeared to be incorrect. The thinned-down eggs must have broken during incubation, and the parent, following normal behavior in that situation, had eaten the contents.

A 1922 photograph showing a small portion of the peregrine egg collection of Karl Pember of Woodstock, Vermont. The five horizontal rows represent five different complete clutches. Note the variations in size, shape, and patterning of eggs laid by different females.   *Karl A. Pember*

Ratcliffe relayed his findings to Dr. Joseph Hickey, Professor of Wildlife Management at the University of Wisconsin, who was studying the decline of peregrine populations in the United States. When Hickey examined thousands of American peregrine eggs, he got very similar results. From Maine to California, also starting in 1947, eggshells had thinned down by an average of almost 19 percent. For some eggs the shell was as much as 26 percent thinner, and shell strength was reduced by 60 percent.

Soon other American scientists experimentally proved in laboratory tests on kestrels that pesticide residues caused thinned-down shells. Even more conclusive were experiments with mallard ducks showing that DDE, the breakdown product of DDT, caused thin shells, a large proportion of cracked or infertile eggs, and a high mortality rate in ducklings that did hatch. Clearly DDT was doing much more than just thinning the shells.

Further research in the laboratory demonstrated that pesticide residues lowered the blood level of estrogen, the female hormone. Thus, sufficient calcium was not reaching the egg that was forming within the mother bird's body, and fragile shells resulted. Furthermore, since estrogen controls the entire female reproductive cycle, the reduction of estrogen levels in the bird's blood probably affected courtship, mating, egg laying, incubation, and care of the young. In 1969, Dr. Tom Cade of Cornell University discovered that a considerable number of Alaskan nestlings had apparently died from exposure or starvation. They had not been brooded or fed, even though the parent birds were at the eyries. Such behavior truly was abnormal, and it raised the specter that in addition to causing fragile shells by blocking the flow of calcium, as well as causing infertility, pesticides may indeed work their hideous effect in much the way that Ratcliffe first suspected when he saw the falcon eating her egg.

The American peregrine was the first bird conclusively shown

43

to have been killed off by pesticides. This revelation led directly to an almost complete ban on DDT by the Federal government in 1970. The American peregrine was declared to be an endangered species. Shooting, trapping, or dealing in peregrines within the United States become a Federal offense. The sad part, of course, is that this protection came too late to save the proud birds that had bred in all those eyries since long before man first watched them.

Are peregrines gone forever from the United States? Will they ever live and breed here again? Some scientists believe they can be brought back. They are breeding peregrines in captivity and attempting to restock the species in the United States as the lingering pesticide residues diminish with the passage of time. To do this work, scientists must be experts in peregrine behavior, in a very practical sense, and highly skilled at handling the birds. Much of what we know about peregrine behavior comes from falconry. Falconers are experts at handling, training, and flying various birds of prey, but no bird has commanded more of their admiration, devotion, and endeavors over hundreds of years than the peregrine.

PART II

Falconry

*T*he ancient art of falconry, hunting with trained birds of prey, probably originated in Persia or China over 4,000 years ago. From there it spread westward into Europe and became extremely popular during the Middle Ages. Emperors, kings, and lesser nobles had elaborate facilities and expert falconers to train and care for their prized birds. A particular kind of bird was assigned to each rank of nobility. Eagles were restricted to the emperor, gyrfalcons were reserved for the king, the noble lady flew the merlin, and so on. However, peregrines were the favorite all-around hunting birds. In addition to having outstanding powers of flight and attack, peregrines could be readily trained to ascend and "wait on," circling in the air above a mounted hunting party until the quarry was flushed into the open. Falconry was highly competitive, with each hunter flying his favorite bird against the others to see which was the most capable hunter and the most beautiful in flight.

Falconry has continued to be practiced right up to the present time. In fact, in recent years the number of falconers in the United States has increased. This increase has created problems, especially since peregrines, always the most sought-after birds, have virtually disappeared as a breeding species in the country. Since they have been declared an endangered species, the trap-

Falconer on horseback. From a Franco-Flemish tapestry
of the early 16th century, *The Hunt of the Unicorn: Return
from the Hunt.*   *The Metropolitan Museum of Art,
Bequest of Helen Hay Whitney, 1945.*

ping or sale of peregrines has been banned by Federal law, and
ownership of the birds is now carefully restricted.

In the future, if peregrines can be reestablished in sufficient
numbers as native-breeding birds, the restrictive laws on trapping, buying, selling, trading, and owning them may be re-
evaluated and modified. Although peregrines are now strictly
protected, prairie falcons, merlins, kestrels, and a variety of

A modern falconer preparing to fly.   *John Kaufmann*

other birds of prey can still be obtained and flown in those states where falconry is permitted by law.

Despite the fact that the number of falconers has grown, falconry is not a popular activity in the United States. There are about four hundred serious, practicing falconers in this country, according to their organization, the North American Falconers Association. The group has always been limited by the difficulties of obtaining, training, flying, and keeping the birds.

To the casual observer, falconry might seem to be a glamorous sport, an exciting hobby to be pursued for fun. However, behind the glamour and the excitement there is a lot of time-consuming, unexciting, hard work. The falconer must have patience, persistence, and dedication. He must be willing to go through long periods of preparing, training, and maintaining his

47

birds in order to fly them for relatively short periods in the field. The flight of a peregrine may last only thirty seconds from the moment of release until the prey is downed. Yet months of work may have preceded the flight. Enthusiastic beginners cannot anticipate the great amount of time and effort required in falconry. Few novices remain interested for long, and when they quit, the birds in their care suffer. Accordingly, experienced and concerned falconers and the North American Falconers Association usually try to discourage newcomers. They stress the fact that falcons are not pets to be caged and kept for show.

Still, a knowledge of falconry and the careful procedures used in training and flying peregrines provides a useful background for understanding and appreciating the efforts now under way to restore one of the greatest of all birds to our cliffs and skies. Although some people may not approve of falconry as such, since it involves hunting one creature with another, anyone who is interested in and concerned about the peregrine should realize that the only chance of bringing it back depends upon the skillful use of the techniques of falconry.

Only young peregrines can be readily trained for falconry, since they have little or no experience in the wild. Therefore, falconers used to take the young birds from the eyrie before they could fly, or they trapped them later as they traveled south on their first fall migration. Young peregrines removed from the eyrie were called *eyesses*.

Taking eyesses was a common practice in earlier times, when falconers did not care how much they disturbed the parent birds' nesting activities. Peregrines were plentiful and seemingly would always be so. As long as the birds were breeding normally in a healthy environment, the effect on the population from the loss of some eyesses was negligible. In England, for example, eyesses had been captured for hundreds of years with no appar-

48

ent drop in the numbers of breeding birds. However, once pesticides began eating away at the peregrine populations, the stealing of eyesses hastened their inevitable disappearance. Some ruthless individuals persisted in robbing the eyries even after they knew that peregrines were rapidly vanishing, although most American falconers did not.

In any case, in terms of practical falconry, eyesses often did not make good hunters. Taken from the scrape before they could fly, they lacked any experience of hunting in the wild. If raised in captivity, they came to associate their feeding with man, became "imprinted" to human beings as their foster parents, and often were much too tame for hunting.

However, there was an old method of raising eyesses so that they learned to fly and hunt on their own and still remained basically wild. This method was called *hacking,* or putting a bird out to hack. It was a difficult, tedious, and lengthy procedure, but it has recently become very important since it is the way peregrines raised in captivity can be returned to the wild. In hacking, the eyesses were placed untethered in an open box on a pole or a high tree stump. They were still not fully developed, so they could not fly at first. Food was raised up on a long stick and placed in the box over the edge, so the birds could not see their human provider. Thus, their instinctive fear of man was preserved, and they continued to be essentially wild.

When the young birds learned to fly, they ventured into the surrounding countryside and instinctively began to attempt hunting wild prey. At first they were unsuccessful without the example of their parents to follow. Usually they needed from six weeks to two months to develop their flying and hunting skills to the point where they killed enough birds to feed themselves. However, they knew where their box was and could always return to find food when they failed to kill. Finally, when they seemed to be fairly self-sufficient, the falconer set his traps, recaptured the birds, and brought them in for training. Since they were still basically wild, they became good hunters.

Nevertheless, putting peregrines out to hack involved a number of problems. First, the method involved a lot of work supplying food and keeping track of the loose birds. Second, there were many chances for human interference, since the birds were flying and roosting overnight near populated areas. The strong likelihood existed that they might be shot. Finally, the birds might always fly off on their own before they could be trapped and taken in for training. However, in countries like Scotland, where there were few opportunities to trap young peregrines on migra-

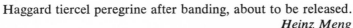

Haggard tiercel peregrine after banding, about to be released.
Heinz Meng

tion, falconry depended upon training eyesses. In Holland, on the other hand, where a main migration pathway funneled through Europe, young migrant peregrines were plentiful and were easily trapped in the open fields and along the beaches.

Even in earlier times adult peregrines, or haggards, captured during migration were banded and released, never kept for falconry. Since adults comprised the active breeding stock, on whom the next generation depended, they were left alone. Then too, like eyesses straight from the eyrie, haggards were generally unsuitable for falconry. They had *too much* experience living and hunting on their own, so they were extremely difficult to handle and train.

The most suitable birds for falconry were young peregrines traveling south on their first fall migration, called *birds of the year,* or *passage peregrines.* Passage peregrines had hunted with their parents and on their own for a couple of months, so their flight and attack were already well developed. When trained in falconry, they retained enough of their independence to make very good hunters.

In the United States, falconers trapped passage peregrines along the Atlantic coastline on sandy offshore islands such as Assateague Island in Maryland. Most of the peregrines passing there came from northern regions—Greenland, Labrador, eastern Canada, and the Canadian tundra. One bird banded at Assateague was later found in Greenland, while another was recovered in Argentina, showing what a vast range they cover. Most of them were tundra peregrines, *Falco peregrinus tundrius,* so trapping them had little effect on the population of *Falco peregrinus anatum,* the American peregrine. Tundra birds continued to show up at Assateague in the same numbers right up through the time when the American peregrine disappeared from the eastern United States.

51

Heinz Meng in 1946. The haggard peregrine was caught with the head set
he holds.   *Heinz Meng*

   Falconers had several different methods for trapping peregrines. One was called the *head set,* in which the falconer lay on
his back, buried in the sand. His head was raised, and he looked
out from a camouflaged covering. When a peregrine came down
and landed on the live pigeon tied to the falconer's hand, he
reached up and grabbed it by the legs.
   Another made use of a trap called the *bow net.* The falconer
hid in a canvas cover or blind, and tethered pigeons lured the
peregrine to land within the net area. The falconer then pulled

A bow-net trap. *John Kaufmann*

the trigger line to release the spring-powered bow net, which instantly snapped up and over, trapping the peregrine.

Still another technique used rectangular nets called *dho-gazza* traps, which the falconer suspended between two poles. He often placed them on either side of a bow net, where they increased the chances of catching a peregrine as it made low passes to investigate. The peregrine hit the net, which pulled loose from the poles, furled over, and trapped the bird.

Sometimes a falconer drove a jeep along the beach, keeping pace with a migrating peregrine, and tossed out the simplest trap of all, known as the *noosed pigeon*. One end of a ball of heavy fishing line was tied to the pigeon. The line unwound upon release of the bird and dragged along the ground, slowing its flight and making it an easy target for the peregrine. Eventually the drag forced the pigeon to land, but before then the peregrine

53

Above: Passage peregrine caught with a noosed pigeon. *Heinz Meng*

Below: After sliding to a stop, Heinz Meng grasps a passage tundra peregrine caught in a chase on the beach. The noosed pigeon can be seen just below the peregrine's feet. *G. Ronald Austing*

usually grabbed, or bound to, the bird and rode it down. The pigeon wore a harness covered with many fine monofilament nooses. When the peregrine stood on the pigeon to feed, its toes became snared in the nooses.

Nooses were also fastened to the outside of a trap called the *bal-chatri,* a wire cage containing a pigeon, which acted as a lure. The bal-chatri was often dropped out onto the ground from a slowly moving car near a migrating peregrine. When the bird landed on the cage, its feet became snared.

As soon as she was caught on the beach, a passage falcon was hooded. Since vision is by far her keenest sense, shutting off her view of things that could frighten her was the best way to calm her. Jesses, thin leather straps, were fastened to her legs and attached with a swivel to a leash. The leash was tied to a block perch, a cylindrical piece of wood, supported on top of a pointed shaft that was stuck into the ground. Since peregrines are ledge nesters, their feet are most comfortable on flat surfaces like the block perch.

Inside a beach shelter shared by falconers in earlier times. Hooded passage peregrines are on transportable screen perches.　　　　　*Heinz Meng*

Right: Peregrine tethered to a block perch with leash, swivel, clips, and jesses.
John Kaufmann

John Kaufmann

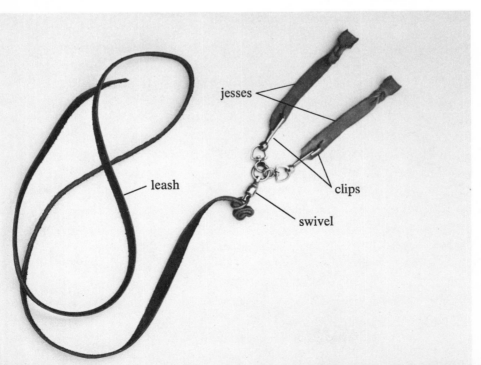

jesses

leash

clips

swivel

Hooded passage peregrine on a screen perch. *Heinz Meng*

The first phase of conditioning a bird for falconry is called *manning*. Manning consists of getting the falcon used to living with the falconer, being fed by him, accepting her new surroundings, and in general losing some of her natural fear of man. Back home, the falconer puts his new bird, still hooded, on a screen perch in his hawk house, or mews. The screen perch, a padded horizontal pole with burlap hanging from it, is used to confine the falcon's movements, to keep her in place and as calm as possible. If she should "bate," jump from the perch with wings fluttering, the jesses will hold her and she will swing down against the burlap screen and hang there by the legs until the falconer lifts her up again. For this reason the falconer makes sure that she is calm and not liable to bate before he leaves her alone. Usually she sits quite calmly on the perch.

The falconer does not feed his new bird the first day. Since he has no way of knowing how much or when she has last eaten, he waits for her to "cast" before he feeds her. When casting, the bird expels from her mouth a cylindrical pellet an inch or two long consisting of densely packed feathers, small pieces of bone, and other indigestible matter. Casting usually takes place early in the morning. A falcon's first hood is designed to allow her to open her beak wide during casting. However, there is another way to solve the problem of casting through the hood. Since the pellet consists of indigestible matter, feeding the hooded bird pigeon breast meat without feathers eliminates the need for casting, which serves no other purpose than getting rid of inert material.

To give his bird her first meal, the falconer approaches her slowly and gently while holding a piece of fresh pigeon meat in his hand. He whistles soft, repeated notes and makes little squeaking sounds by drawing air in through his closed lips. The falcon soon learns to associate these sounds with the arrival of the falconer and the feeding that follows. Later on in the field he will use these same sounds to draw her attention from her downed prey in order to coax her up onto his glove.

When approaching a hooded bird to feed her for the first time, the falconer also plays with her toes, stroking and pinching them lightly. Sensing that something is alive and moving down there, the bird will hiss and bring her beak down to bite the unseen thing that is bothering her. In doing so, she bites into the meat the falconer holds ready, then proceeds to eat.

On the second evening in dim light, holding the meat in front of the hooded bird, touching her toes, whistling and squeaking, the falconer coaxes her onto his glove. He rests his gloved hand

Falconer picking up hooded peregrine from screen perch.   *John Kaufmann*

on his knee to steady his arm and make her feel more secure. He squats in a clear area where the bird cannot injure her wings if she bates and flutters in fright. The falcon starts to feed. When she has eaten about a third of the meat, the falconer loosens and lifts off her hood. This is her first sight of him and her surroundings since capture. Since the light is very low the bird cannot see clearly, so she does not become startled.

The falconer holds his bird steady while she feeds and becomes accustomed to the situation. Then as she is about to eat the last gulp, he hoods her once again. He does not allow her to finish feeding, then hood her, because she would associate hooding with the disappearance of food and would resist it. After dark, the falconer removes the hood so the falcon will be less constrained during the night. Accordingly, he must get up very early for the first few days, in order to go out and rehood his bird before it gets light.

As the bird begins to get used to her surroundings and to the falconer, he does not have to hood her before it grows light. If she seems calm on the perch, the falconer may wait for some time as daylight increases and allow her to adjust to the sight of her new home and to himself as he enters the hawk house. "Intention movements" become especially important at this time. For instance, if the bird stiffens up as the falconer approaches, he does not stop in his tracks, but slows down gradually and moves off to one side while she regains her composure. He avoids all abrupt movements. So when the falconer enters the hawk house by daylight, he moves gradually and on his glove carries some meat, which he feeds his bird as he hoods her. The hood serves to calm the falcon during her first days. As she becomes used to the hawk house, the falconer leaves her unhooded while she is there.

Falconer approaching peregrine on screen perch.   *John Kaufmann*

Soon the falcon learns to come readily to the glove for food. When the falconer holds up a piece of meat, she jumps from her perch onto his glove. Before long these jumps can be extended to short flights, called *flying to the fist*. The falcon, unleashed and waiting on her perch, takes off, flies across the room, and lands on the gloved fist.

The falconer keeps his new bird indoors for about a week. This confinement is necessary because she has been captured during migration and so would respond to the various stimuli of migration, including the sight of other birds flying south, if she

Passage peregrine flying to the fist.   *G. Ronald Austing*

Heinz Meng's yard at New Paltz, showing peregrines outdoors on block perches, with bath pans nearby. *John Kaufmann*

were allowed unhooded outdoors. Once her routine has been redirected to center around the falconer and the food he brings her, she can be brought outside for a limited time. So on a sunny day the falconer gives his bird a piece of meat, takes her outdoors on his glove, and places her on a block perch. According to whether she is nervous or calm, he may or may not use the hood while moving her. A wide, shallow pan filled with water is placed near the perch for her to bathe in.

The falconer feeds his bird, moves away slowly, and sits down nearby. The falcon scrapes her beak with her talons or wipes it on the side of the perch to clean off the scraps of meat. She may then jump down and bathe by splashing herself in the water. Afterward she spends time preening her feathers. If she seems calm and is sitting well, the falconer may leave her outside for the rest of the afternoon to "weather," or get used to her outdoor surroundings. But if she is nervous and starts to bate and flutter, he hoods her and puts her back inside. When she calms down, he leaves her there unhooded. Eventually, after she is fully trained, the only time the hood is used is when the falcon is being transported out to the field to fly. Then it serves primarily to eliminate sights that would distract her before she is ready to be released into flight.

Once the hood is no longer needed in the hawk house, the falconer may dispense with the screen perch and use the recently invented shelf perches. These perches give the leashed falcon enough freedom to jump down to a landing ledge and up again, allowing her some indoor exercise. The perches are covered with rug to protect the bird's talons, and the ledge is covered with soft litter material.

Passage peregrine on shelf perch.   *Heinz Meng*

The falconer may choose to do without the screen perch altogether by using a shelf perch right at the start of manning. If the hooded bird bates from the shelf perch, she simply comes down on the soft material atop the ledge and stays there until the falconer puts her up on the shelf again. This procedure completely eliminates the possibility of the falcon hanging by her heels.

Falconers of old believed that the more time they spent on manning a bird, the better hunter she would make. They took their birds with them everywhere for many days and even carried them on the glove right into church. Modern falconers regard this prolonged manning as completely outmoded and based on nothing but tradition and superstition. The way a bird is manned is much more important than the total hours spent. Gentle, patient, self-assured handling, which develops the bird's normal routine and is directed toward her future activities, is what really counts. Manning is not an inflexible program to be followed to the letter; it requires judgment, flexibility, and above all a feeling for the bird. When properly done, manning a peregrine should take no more than about ten days. After that time the falconer starts training his bird to fly to the lure.

The lure is a dummy quarry, which the falconer uses to attract his bird. The best modern lures consist of a wire framework filled with spongy plastic foam. This shape is then covered with nylon and coated with liquid latex. To this basic form are sewed the wings of a pigeon, pheasant, grouse, duck—whatever quarry the falcon will be trained to hunt.

A leash attached to the lure allows the falconer to swing it through the air to attract the falcon. The lure is then thrown out on the ground, and the falcon lands on it. In much the same way that a wild peregrine will carry off its downed prey if it is not too large and heavy, an untrained falcon may try to lift and fly off with the lure. The leash, trailing a four-ounce weight behind,

Pheasant lures, showing leash with weight attached. *Heinz Meng*

normally provides enough drag to prevent such an effort. However, certain peregrines have a strong tendency to pick up and
carry a lure. In these cases, the falconer may use a weighted lure
of about a half pound to discourage carrying. The weighted lure
is used only during the first part of training and is only thrown
out a short distance onto the ground. Caution is necessary, since
if a falcon were to strike at a weighted lure in midair, the impact
could be fatal.

In the first stage of training, the peregrine simply learns to
come to the lure for food. The falconer teaches her by "garnish-
ing" the lure—attaching meat to it—and throwing it out onto the
ground a short distance away as the bird flies out from a perch.
During this period the falcon is attached by her jesses to what is
called a *creance,* a nylon line tied at its other end to a stick about
a foot long and two inches in diameter. If the bird should try to
fly away, the stick drags along the ground and slows her flight
until she lands and the falconer can retrieve her. When training
is done properly, however, the falcon is hardly aware that she

Prairie falcon on creance, flying to the lure.   *Heinz Meng*

is not flying free. A block perch is set up in a smooth, flat area such as an athletic field, where the creance cannot get caught and injure the bird by stopping her short.

To start, the falconer moves about ten yards away from his bird as she sits unhooded on the perch. He walks with his back to the falcon so as not to attract her immediately with sight of the lure he is holding. The bells attached to her feet will ring if she starts off the perch before he is ready, warning him to turn quickly. At the proper distance the falconer turns, calls "ho!" swings the lure in a circle to show it to the falcon, and throws it out onto the ground a short distance away. She flies out, lands on the lure, and starts to feed. The falconer lets her eat some of the meat, then uses another piece to coax her back onto his glove. The next flights are made over longer distances until the falcon will come readily to the lure at fifty yards.

Next an ungarnished lure is used, as the bird flies out over longer distances on the creance. Now when the falcon lands on the lure, she finds no meat. The falconer comes out to her. He

66

brings his hand down with some meat concealed beneath it. Then he exposes the meat and allows her to eat some of it as he takes her up on his glove. By now she has begun to learn the sequence leading up to her being fed. She first takes the lure, then waits for the falconer to bring food. Before long, when hunting, she will even learn that waiting for the rich, red meat the falconer brings is easier than plucking her downed prey. However, if he takes too long to reach her after she makes her kill, she will start plucking and eating. This is desirable, since it keeps her occupied and in one place until the falconer arrives.

Once the falcon comes well to the ungarnished lure, the next step is to fly her free. The falconer waits for a calm day, so that if his bird flies off, the wind will not carry her far. On the previous day he has fed her about half the normal amount, so she is somewhat hungry. This condition gives her an extra incentive to come when he swings the lure.

The free-flying falcon springs up from her perch, the falconer swings the lure in a circle, then drops it to the ground, but keeps hold of the end of the leash. As the falcon heads toward the lure and is about to land, the falconer pulls it up and away from her. The falcon keeps flying and passes by, still looking for the lure. She banks up and around again toward the falconer, since she knows that he has the food. On the next pass the falconer throws out the lure and lets her take it on the ground. The first day he feeds her after making one pass, the next day he leads her through two passes, and so on, gradually increasing the length of her flights.

If his peregrine has been fully trained for lure flying, the falconer can delay until she has taken off, "ringed up" in a spiral climb to her maximum height, or "pitch," and is circling overhead, or "waiting on" before he shows her the lure. When she comes down swiftly to make her pass, the falconer swings the

lure rapidly in circles. As she heads in to grab it, he pulls it away from her path at the last instant. He leads her through a number of passes this way and finally looses the lure upward as she flies by, so that she can bind to it in midair. She then either lets it fall, circles around and down and lands on top of it, or binds to it and glides with it to the ground.

Lure flying becomes an art in itself as the falconer performs with style and grace, smoothly coordinating his movements with the low, swooping passes of a well-trained peregrine. Some peregrines are especially trained for lure flying and are seldom used for hunting. Others may be good lure fliers and may also be flown against pigeons or game birds that the falconer releases.

Opposite, top: Swinging the lure.

Opposite, bottom: Releasing the lure.

Below: Peregrine binding to the lure.   *John Kaufmann*

Still others may be used almost exclusively for hunting wild game, with an occasional flight after released quarry.

The lure is important and useful in all aspects of falconry, including hunting wild game. For example, once a peregrine is flying free after quarry, she may go off on a "tail chase," a fast, direct pursuit across the fields. If her prey outflies her and escapes, the falcon may land in a tree or on a pole. The falconer can usually bring her down just by standing out in the open, calling to her, and swinging the lure. Well-trained peregrines usually come to the swinging lure; they will sometimes come to it even when they are far aloft out of sight. If the lure alone does not work, the falconer may tether a live pigeon to the leash, swing the fluttering bird, then release it up into the air. The pigeon starts to fly off, but after a few moments the leash with the four-ounce weight attached begins to slow it to a halt. Few peregrines can resist coming down to such a stimulating target.

The performance of a well-trained bird depends more than anything else on how its feeding is regulated. A thorough knowledge of when and how much to feed his birds is the mark of the expert falconer. Falconers underfeed their birds the day before flying them in order to make them "keen," to stoop well after the lure or to pursue their live quarry with determination. However, the extra incentive that hunger gives a bird must always be weighed against the effect on its physical condition.

Keeping a bird too hungry may produce exactly the opposite effect from the one intended. First, its style of flight and overall performance will be hampered, because a hungry bird is so keen that it will not ring up to a high pitch and make long stoops. Instead, it will make very short stoops from a low height and act like a hungry dog at its master's heels at feeding time. The expert falconer aims to get his peregrine "high," literally soaring up as far as possible, while still controlling the flight. To perform this way, the bird must be fed enough to be in excellent physical condition so it will feel strong and free enough to fly in grand style.

A much more serious result of underfeeding is that it can drastically weaken a bird by depleting its energy reserves, which are mainly stored as fat in the breast tissues. Since the bird burns energy at a very high rate and needs frequent replenishment, underfeeding can weaken it so rapidly that it may suddenly die with little apparent warning. For this reason, falconers constantly check the energy reserve of the birds they are flying by weighing them and by pushing aside the breast feathers to examine the fat deposits underneath the skin.

Weighing a peregrine. *Heinz Meng*

Peregrine flight feathers ready for storage after the completion of molting. On the left is a complete set of tail feathers; on the right the outer three primary feathers from each wing.   *John Kaufmann*

Maintaining adequate energy reserves is also a problem during the peregrine's yearly molt, when worn flight feathers fall out and new ones grow in to replace them. Peregrine molt is more gradual than that of most other birds, which replace more flight feathers at the same time, since a high degree of flying performance is not so crucial to their feeding. Peregrine molt lasts roughly from April to October. During this time most falconers "put up" their birds by either not flying them at all or flying them in a very limited way.

Growing new feathers causes a heavy drain on the bird's energy reserves. In the wild this condition is no problem, since a peregrine can simply eat more to make up for it. With falcons in captivity, however, it can cause difficulties, because the falconer controls the bird's flight performance by withholding a certain amount of food. An insufficient food supply during molt causes structural defects in the flight feathers, which show up as light lines running across the webs. Under the stress of hard flying, these weak feathers will break. So by putting up their birds and feeding them fully, falconers can be sure they will have all the nutrients necessary for growing perfect feathers.

If a bird damages a wing or tail feather, a new one does not grow in until the next yearly molt. Damaged feathers affect a peregrine's flying performance. To deal with this problem, the falconer labels and stores each flight feather as it drops off during molt. If the falcon later damages a feather, the falconer has someone help him hold the bird steady while he cuts down the old feather and fastens on a matching feather to replace it. This technique is called *imping*. To imp a feather, the falconer cuts down the original shaft, leaving about an inch at the base. He inserts a plastic, metal, or wooden pin halfway into the soft core of the shaft stump and cements it with epoxy into place. He cuts the replacement feather to fit, then cements it to the other end of the pin. Since the pin is flexible, the substitute feather can bend as it naturally would.

Falconry originated in the pursuit of wild game using trained birds, and hunting is still the ultimate form of falconry. All the other procedures, from trapping, manning, and lure flying, to the careful maintenance of the birds by feeding, imping, and so on, are really preparations for this most difficult aspect of the ancient art. Hunting is the crucial test of falcon and falconer.

There are two main types of hunting in falconry. In the first, game hawking, the falcon is released to climb and wait on overhead while her wild prey is flushed from cover on the ground. As in medieval times, hunting dogs are sometimes used to locate

Above: Peregrine waiting on.   *G. Ronald Austing*

Below: Passage falcon with pheasant she has just killed.   *Heinz Meng*

the wild game and flush it from cover. Game birds such as partridge, pheasant, or quail, ordinarily stay on the ground under cover or not far from cover. When flushed, they put on a quick burst of speed to escape. They fly fast, but they don't fly long or far before taking cover again. Thus, they will not lead a falcon on a long cross-country chase where the falconer may lose her.

Pigeons can fly fast and far. With sufficient lead, a pigeon may try to outfly a peregrine. Pigeons are very strong fliers, especially when fleeing for their lives. In level flight against the wind, when a peregrine's larger wing area retards its speed, a strong pigeon can outfly a peregrine. However, even if the peregrine does finally catch up with the pigeon and make the kill, the long tail chase may have carried her far beyond the falconer's sight. The same problem arises when peregrines are flown against ducks in inaccessible marsh areas.

Peregrine closing in on a pigeon.   *John Kaufmann*

Above, top: Falcon with downed pigeon she has plucked while the falconer was delayed in reaching her during a long tail chase.　　*John Kaufmann*

Above: Falconer moving in slowly to pick up his bird. Woolen glove substitutes for leather one dropped during chase.　　*John Kaufmann*

Below: Falcon back on the glove, feeding on her prey.　　*John Kaufmann*

Above, top: Passage peregrine with pigeon killed in winter game hawking.
Heinz Meng

Above: Heinz Meng with a peregrine that won first prize in hunting competition at the North American Falconers Association field trials, 1971.
George Laycock

The other type of hunting, flying from the fist, is more difficult than game hawking for both falcon and falconer. The falcon is carried hooded on the glove. The falconer sights the prey, unhoods the falcon, and "slips," or releases, her at the prey. The prey spots the falcon at some distance and starts to escape. Thus, the prey has more warning of the approaching attack. Also, the falcon does not have the great initial advantage of waiting on overhead, ready to stoop. She must either gain some pitch during the pursuit and stoop from a low height or simply fly fast and hard to overtake her prey. Slipping the falcon at the right moment and position calls for quick decisions, and the flights are much less predictable and controllable than those of game hawking. The falconer relies more upon the merits of his bird.

Regardless of what kind of hunting she will do, a new falcon is "entered," or released for the first time after quarry, once she has had about ten days of training to the lure. She is entered on the particular kind of quarry she will hunt. This first exposure is very important. If he enters his bird on one kind of prey, then later flies her against another kind, the falconer runs a greater risk of losing her. For instance, if a peregrine is entered on pigeons and starts hunting them, then is later flown against ducks, she is always liable to "check," or turn away from her intended quarry, to chase some pigeon flying half a mile off.

Entering a peregrine. The falconer releases a pigeon as the falcon waits on overhead. *John Kaufmann*

Peregrines have been flown from the fist against a number of birds that they also hunt in the wild, such as starlings and pigeons. One bird the wild peregrine seldom hunts is the crow. There are a number of reasons for this avoidance beside the traditional one that crow meat is very unpalatable. The clever, wary crow lives cooperatively in flocks. Spotter crows act as lookouts for the flock by stationing themselves apart and cawing in alarm when danger threatens. Thus, crows are hard to approach by surprise and usually have sufficient warning time to flee from feeding in open fields to take cover in nearby woods. Under attack, crows are very skillful dodgers, shifting abruptly at the very last instant so the attacker often misses completely.

The crow is a fairly large and strong bird. When downed but not stunned, it will put up a tough fight, grabbing tenaciously and jabbing with its sharp beak. It will keep calling, and its flock will respond to the cries by ganging up on the attacker and driving it off. The crow is very difficult prey, even for the peregrine, and for this reason crow hawking is a great challenge. Not many falconers have practiced it, but those who have claim that there is no greater test of falcon and falconer.

Crow lure. *John Kaufmann*

Passage peregrine standing on a crow lure.   *Heinz Meng*

The falconer trains his peregrine for crow hawking by using a large black lure fitted with crow wings. To enter his bird, he waits for a calm day and makes the first slip from as short a distance as possible, to give her a good chance to make her first kill and so encourage her. He uses his car as a moving blind to enable him to approach the feeding crows much closer than he could on foot.

The falconer spots three crows feeding about 150 yards away on a hillside. He approaches slowly in his car, takes his falcon on his fist, unhoods her, and slips her through the car window. She spots the crows, they spot her, and the chase is on, with the peregrine flying uphill all the way. Beating hard and fast, she gains quickly on the flapping, squawking birds. Just as they are about to duck into the cover of some trees, she singles out one crow and stoops swiftly. With a burst of black feathers the crow tumbles to the ground. The falcon spirals down after it, pounces on the stunned crow, and severs its neck. Suddenly, calling a loud cry of revenge, about fifty crows fly out from the trees and begin to mob the falcon, milling around her, diving and darting with jabbing beaks. Running up the hill at top speed, the falconer reaches his bird just in time to keep the flock from driving her off. A minute's delay on his part, and her successful entry in

80

Crow hawking. *John Kaufmann*

grand style would have turned into a desperate retreat. If a falcon is mobbed on her entering flight, she will probably never hunt crows again.

Hunting flights do not follow a set plan. There are always surprises. The falcon's condition and determination, her sighting and chasing alternate prey, the quarry's behavior, changes in wind speed and direction are just a few of the things that make for endless variety. However, because of the uncertainties, losing a peregrine remains a constant possibility, even for the expert. If his bird comes down out of sight but within hearing range, the falcon's bells can help to locate her. But if she lands too far out of sight, finding her can be very difficult and sometimes impossible.

Hunting.   *G. Ronald Austing*

To help retrieve a lost bird, modern falconers can use a system of radiotelemetry. This equipment consists of a miniature radio transmitter that the peregrine wears on one leg to replace her bells. The transmitter broadcasts a signal with a range of about eight miles and will continue signaling for about two weeks. To locate a peregrine that has landed out of sight, the falconer simply turns his receiver antenna, picks up the signal direction, and follows it out to his bird.

In earlier years falconers flew their peregrines much more freely. Long, adventurous flights with the falcons ringing up and out of sight were not uncommon and were the most exhilarating part of falconry. Today, with peregrines so scarce, even if they can afford expensive radiotelemetry equipment, falconers are

82

Above: Radio transmitter fastened to a peregrine's leg with antenna wire trailing down.   *Robert Demetry*

Below: Heinz Meng with the receiver antenna, listening to a peregrine's transmitter signal.   *John Kaufmann*

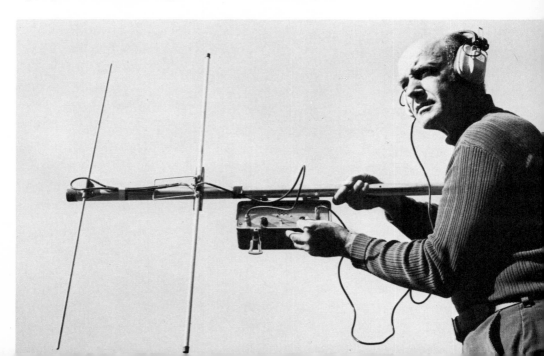

very reluctant to take chances with their birds. Very few of them, for example, would now subject a peregrine to the rigorous trials of crow hawking.

By the early 1960's, when scientists were coming to realize that pesticides had decimated the peregrine throughout much of North America, a number of people turned their attention to something that had been tried in the past but had almost always failed: the breeding of peregrines in captivity. If DDT and other hard pesticides could be outlawed, there might eventually be some hope that peregrines raised in an uncontaminated environment could be returned to the wild to live and breed once again on those cliffs that had fallen silent. Falconer-ornithologists led the way in this endeavor.

PART III

Falcons Return

*O*n a clear, cool October day in 1941 a young man and his father are surf casting in the Atlantic at Jones Beach on Long Island, New York. The fishing is very slow, so the young man, Heinz Meng, decides to hike back through the sand dunes to see what birds and insects can be found. The autumn migration is still under way. Many birds, monarch butterflies, and dragonflies are passing, all going south down the Atlantic coast.

Suddenly Meng spies some feathers wafting up and out from behind a dune. Is a hawk plucking its kill? He creeps up slowly and glances over the sandy rise. A short distance away a peregrine is crouched over a marsh hawk it has just killed, plucking the breast, looking up, then plucking again. Meng gradually slips off his jacket, creeps closer and closer, then throws it over the peregrine. The bird thrashes beneath the jacket, but he subdues it and takes it home. Although he is a complete novice at falconry, Meng starts to train the peregrine. Before long, however, a barking dog frightens the bird during a training flight and it flies away. Meng is very disappointed, but by now he has made up his mind to become a falconer.

Long before the incident with the peregrine, Heinz Meng had shown a strong and constant love of birds, and especially birds of prey. In his teens he acquired a copy of *The Book of Bird*

Peregrine and eyrie with young (at lower left), Taughannock Falls, near Ithaca, New York, 1925.   *Arthur A. Allen*

Life by the late Professor Arthur Allen. The frontispiece was the picture shown on this page, a peregrine eyrie at Taughannock Falls near Ithaca, New York, where Professor Allen taught at Cornell University. Meng was fascinated by the sight of the young birds in the eyrie and the parent perched against the cascading waterfall in the background. Largely because of this photograph, he had decided to study ornithology at Cornell. Catching the peregrine, therefore, came as a dramatic climax to the early influences on Meng's choice of career.

At Cornell, Meng practiced some falconry with various birds of prey but was unable to spend much time at it until 1951, when he started teaching at the college of the State University of New York at New Paltz, where today he is a professor of biology. Just west of New Paltz lie the Shawangunk Mountains, where Meng found two peregrine eyries. He visited them each spring to observe the parent birds and band the young. A responsible falconer, he left the nestlings and their parents alone and trapped passage peregrines along the coast during the fall migration.

86

Falcons Return

For a long time, Meng had been interested in caring for and raising various birds of prey. His red-tailed hawk earned her name Mamma Red-Tail by raising young redtails, prairie falcons, and goshawks that Meng placed in her care. She even hatched a chicken and raised it. Under Meng's expert care she

Below: Heinz Meng and Mamma Red-Tail.　　　　　　*Heinz Meng*

Bottom: Mamma Red-Tail feeding a chicken she hatched and raised.
　　　　　　　　　　　　　　　　　　　　　　　　Heinz Meng

has reached the amazing age of twenty-nine years, while the oldest previously known wild redtail lived only thirteen years.

Long experience with this redtail and other birds of prey impressed Meng with their flexibility in adapting to new and unusual situations in captivity. Along with keeping peregrines and other species for falconry, he had developed great skill in caring for young hawks as they grew from nestlings to adults, and in nursing sick and injured birds that people brought to him.

Meng's constant contact, day after day, with peregrines, merlins, Cooper's hawks, goshawks, and various other species, gave him a sense of ease and self-confidence in handling birds of prey. The handler's assurance is very important, since his or her state of mind is communicated to the creature being cared for by such things as steadiness of hand or smoothness of movement. Meng developed a rapport with his birds by living with them every day. Earlier at Cornell, he had spent days searching for nests when he was studying the Cooper's hawk. He came to the point where he moved through the woods "like a Cooper's hawk" and

Heinz Meng with a female Cooper's hawk.   *John Kaufmann*

could sense where a nest might be. So in addition to the formal scientific knowledge of the ornithologist, Meng brought something even more important to his work with peregrines—an intimate and intuitive feeling for his birds, an empathy for them. Meng himself describes this as "thinking like a bird," or "being a bird brain."

After 1957, the two peregrine eyries on the Shawangunk ridge that Meng had observed for a number of years were deserted. He became more and more aware of the widespread, catastrophic decline of the American peregrine as reports came in from falconers in other parts of the United States. Although peregrines from the north were still plentiful during migration along the Atlantic coast, this fact was little consolation for the accelerating disappearance of a great bird from regions of our country where it had lived for countless years.

In the early 1960's, Meng began to think of trying to breed peregrines in captivity. When he asked other falconers about this possibility, most of them thought the idea was crazy. They assumed it was impossible because peregrine courtship behavior involved long, towering flights and tall, steep cliffs, conditions that could not be duplicated in a captive situation.

However, Renz Waller, a famous German falconer, had succeeded in breeding some peregrines in the early 1940's. A few other falconers, most notably Frank Beebe in British Columbia, were attempting to breed peregrines, so Meng decided to try.

In 1964, he designed and built a breeding chamber to adjoin his backyard hawk house. With high hopes he installed a pair of 1964 passage peregrines. By 1967, when the birds were almost of breeding age, they had given little sign of courtship or mating. Meng had begun to wonder if passage birds were the best ones to use for breeding. Since they were already fairly wild and independent when captured, they might be less suitable than eyesses

Heinz Meng's breeding facility at New Paltz, New York, with the hawk house (left) and breeding chambers.   *Heinz Meng*

taken at a young age and raised in captivity. The tame eyesses might have less resistance to mating and producing young in the artificial situation of captivity. In 1967, Meng got the opportunity to try this other approach, when through David Hancock and Frank Beebe he obtained a pair of Peale's peregrine eyesses from the Queen Charlotte Islands in British Columbia.

To accommodate the second peregrine pair, Meng divided his original breeding chamber into two halves. He placed the Peale's peregrines in chamber A and the passage peregrines in chamber B. Each chamber measured fifteen feet in length, fifteen feet in width, and ten feet in height at the eaves. Each had a large south window with two wide shelves so the peregrines could sun themselves as they do for long periods in the wild. A bath pan was provided on the lower shelf. Another window opening faced north and the top half of it was covered with burlap to shield the high-perching birds from the north wind during cold spells. The window areas were covered with vertical aluminum bars. The bars were covered on the outside with wire-mesh screens to pre-

90

vent the falcons from escaping, in case they might squeeze between the bars.

Meng designed the interior space to be large enough for very short flights, so the birds could get adequate exercise, but small enough to prevent them from gaining too much speed and crashing against the walls or ceiling. He covered the rafters, which the birds used for perching, and the window shelves with rug or Astroturf to prevent damage to the peregrines' feet during their frequent landings.

Peale's peregrines in the breeding chamber. The male is below on the feeding shelf.   *Heinz Meng*

A two-foot-wide nesting ledge ran along one end of each chamber, ten feet above the floor. Both were covered with sand to simulate a natural ledge surface. In chamber A the Peale's peregrines had an extra shelf perch up at the top of the breeding chamber. That was the entire physical setup, two small rooms with sandy ledges and perches toward the top, which Meng believed could substitute for the peregrine's natural breeding environment.

Because Hancock and Beebe were concerned that the birds they were providing might escape during flying sessions, they insisted that the Peale's peregrines should not be flown free. Would the fact that the birds had never really flown affect their ability to breed? Meng did not believe that either courtship flights or any normal flying were essential to peregrine breeding. After manning and weathering the Peale's eyesses for two months, he put them in the breeding chamber.

Female peregrines generally do not lay eggs until their fourth year, so they cannot breed before that. Thus, Meng had to devote a great deal of time and care to breeding experiments with no guarantee of any success. After the passage pair reached breeding age, he kept hoping each year for some results. Although the birds showed a few signs of courtship behavior, they never mated. Sometimes the female bird will lay eggs but the pair fails to mate, so the eggs are not fertilized. But Meng's passage female had still not produced *any* eggs by April 1970, after six years. At that time Meng replaced her with Lil, an eight-year-old female lent him by Dr. James Enderson of Colorado College. Lil had laid eggs the year before.

Early one morning Meng saw the passage male fly up to Lil and try to mate. She called repeatedly with her head down and her tail raised, the normal mating posture. However, the attempt did not succeed, and both birds flew up to the ledge out of

92

Meng's view. The next morning he climbed up to check the ledge and found an egg.

Lil had been trapped in Wyoming in mid-August, when she was only about four weeks out of the nest. Her experience in the wild, therefore, was relatively short, and she had adapted to her captive surroundings to the point where she showed normal courtship behavior and laid eggs. Knowing this, Meng's hopes were raised that the Peale's peregrines, which had never fended for themselves, might prove to be more successful breeders than any of the passage birds.

Meng saw the male attempt to mate with Lil a number of times, but each time he stopped and landed on the perch next to her. Lil laid four eggs altogether. One, a strange white egg, lay broken on the floor. She incubated the three remaining eggs. Meng waited several days before disturbing her. Then he climbed up to the nesting ledge to try to see if the eggs were developing.

By shining a strong beam of light through the translucent shell, it is possible to detect development within an incubated egg. This is called *candling,* since that was the light source used in earlier times. An infertile, undeveloped egg shows nothing except the plain pale outline of the yolk and an adjoining air space. If the egg has been fertilized and an embryo is developing, a slightly darker area may be seen within the yolk outline. As the embryo develops further, this spot becomes darker and larger. Finally the outline of the growing chick's head, body, legs, and wings can be seen.

Meng first candled one of the eggs with a large flashlight, but could see nothing. He took the egg into his darkroom and candled it with the much brighter light of a slide projector. A pale area about the size of his thumbnail showed up, but nothing else. The next day, after twelve full days of incubation, he checked all three eggs with the slide projector but could see only the out-

93

line of the yolks, no embryos. He opened up the eggs to be sure and found that all three were infertile. After six years of trying, he had no results to show. At this point, he decided to give up altogether on the passage birds. The Peale's peregrines were already showing some signs of courtship behavior by the end of their third summer. In 1971, they would reach their full breeding age of four years, so Meng decided to concentrate on them.

In February, 1971, high, sharp calls normally heard over the sea cliffs of British Columbia started to ring out through the windows of the small backyard building in New Paltz. On February 24, Meng spotted the male Peale's peregrine sitting on the nest ledge. The following day both male and female were on the ledge with their bodies plumped down in the brooding posture. At feeding time the male carried food up to the female. All the while both birds called out loudly again and again.

A mutual courtship display on the nesting ledge. As the male on the left bows deeply, the female lowers her head and raises her tail. These northern *anatum* peregrines bred successfully in 1973 and 1974 at John Campbell's facilities, Black Diamond, Alberta, Canada.   *R. Wayne Nelson*

Male Peale's peregrine defending his breeding territory, trying to attack intruders through the cage bars.   *Heinz Meng*

On February 25, the male was screaming even louder. Both birds were sitting on the nesting ledge calling loudly, and again the male carried food up to the female. On February 26, both birds sat on the ledge calling, then clucking softly. The male would jump onto the ledge, sit for a few moments to show her where the nesting place was, then jump off again. He strutted in his mating posture with legs straightened, head and tail down, the covert feathers beneath his tail lowered. The female held her corresponding posture, head down low, tail raised high, undertail coverts lowered.

Now the male became very aggressive, even when Meng was outside the breeding chamber. He would dash down, strike the window bars, and hang on the wire mesh with eyes glaring, screaming defiantly as Meng put food on the window shelf. To further stimulate this aggressive breeding behavior and to give

95

the male more confidence in guarding his "territory," Meng cowered away from him each time after leaving the food. This simulation of the act of driving an intruder away from the eyrie was intended to help the male feel bolder and to put him in the proper mood and physiological condition for successful mating.

Mating. The male balances himself above by flapping his wings. Photographed in May, 1973, at the Canadian Wildlife Service's Endangered Species Facilities, Wainwright, Alberta.   *R. Wayne Nelson*

By March 10, the female had laid four eggs and was incubating. Now, as he would in the wild, the male brought food to her. When Meng gave him a pigeon breast, he plucked most of the feathers from it, then carried it up to her on the ledge. He also cached food in various corners of the ledge, tucking it away as if he soon expected the arrival of extra mouths to feed. However, when Meng candled the eggs on March 16, he saw no sign of life within the shells. When he opened them up to check, he found nothing but yolks—all four eggs were infertile.

Peregrines usually lay a second clutch of eggs if the first one is removed or destroyed. The pair "recycles," courting and mating again within a very short time. The Peale's peregrines now seemed to be doing just that. They called frequently and loudly, their undertail coverts were lowered, and the male again carried food up to the ledge. On March 29, just thirteen days after Meng removed the first clutch, the first egg of the second clutch appeared.

On March 31, there was a hopeful sign. As the female bent over the ledge screaming at Meng, the male landed right by her and tried to scramble up onto her back. Thereafter, Meng stayed out of the breeding chamber for some time so as not to disturb the pair. On April 12, he went out early and saw the male incubating and making soft, scraping sounds as he turned the eggs with his beak. Such turning prevents the embryos from attaching themselves to the membrane that lines the inside of the shell.

On May 8, as the female came down off the ledge to take food, Meng heard peeping sounds from at least two chicks. He did not climb up to check, since once again he did not want to interfere. On May 10, he went out to the breeding chamber at 7 a.m. He heard no peeping and thought the chicks might have already been fed, since there had been plenty of food in the chamber. He climbed up to the ledge. Two of the chicks lay

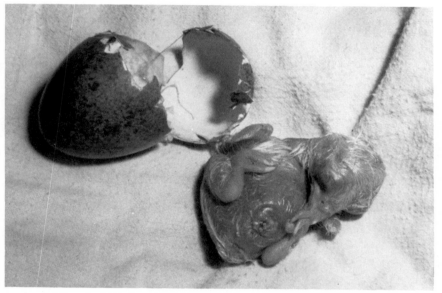

Above, top: Peregrine egg about to hatch, May 10, 1971.   *Heinz Meng*

Above: Peregrine chick (Prince Philip), just hatched, May 19, 1971.
                                                    Heinz Meng

dead, another seemed to be dying, while a fourth was just starting to hatch. The parents had not fed them.

Meng took the egg into his kitchen and watched it hatch at
about 2 p.m. The special egg tooth on the chick's beak punched
its way through the remaining portion of the shell, which parted

as the wet, bedraggled creature with eyes partly closed hunched up and awkwardly pushed its way into the world outside. As soon as the chick was free of the shell, Meng offered it some pieces of pigeon breast meat with a forceps, and the chick eagerly ate them.

The other chick would not eat. It seemed to have an infection in its abdomen. That evening Meng force-fed it, but the next day the food was still lodged in its crop. Meng then tried to give the chick sugar water mixed with an antibiotic, but the failing little creature could not keep the liquid in its stomach. At about noon the chick died.

As the last survivor of the second clutch, the healthy chick must have had good fortune on its side. Since the parents had not been feeding their offspring, it too would probably have died if Meng had waited a day or two longer before checking the ledge. He fed the little peregrine cut-up day-old chicks and pigeon breast meat. The downy little creature looked so awkward that he could hardly believe it would turn into one of the sleekest of all birds. Every now and then it would sit up, but usually it would lie on its stomach, stretch out its legs, and flap its stumpy featherless wings.

Meng tended to his precious newborn chick like an anxious father. For the first couple of weeks he fed it on demand, every two hours, day and night. Afterward he fed it the last meal at 11 p.m. before he went to bed; then he hurried out again in the dark at 5 a.m. to refill its empty crop. By May 14, four days after hatching, the chick sat up now and then, preened its down, and seemed to enjoy the touch of Meng's hand sheltering it from above. By May 16, it was sitting up more often, preening and spreading its wings. By this time too, its leg muscles were stronger, and soon its legs stayed together beneath its body instead of spreading out wide.

Heinz Meng feeding Prince Philip, about three days old.
Chris Farlekas

Meng watched his young peregrine grow and develop, eagerly observing how fast the wing primary feathers sprouted, and checking all the other minute details he had never been able to observe before. On the thirteenth day he determined that "it" was a tiercel and named him Prince Philip, since both his parents were British subjects, since his peregrine lineage gave him noble rank, and since England's Prince Philip has been active in wild-life conservation. Newspaper and magazine articles appeared telling about Meng's successful raising of a peregrine in captivity. After Prince Philip had acquired his full immature plumage, Meng took him around when lecturing on raising peregrines and the future possibility of reviving the species within its former nesting range in the United States.

100

Above: Prince Philip, thirty-three days old.   *Heinz Meng*

Below: Prince Philip in adult plumage.   *Ralph S. Palmer*

Although Meng was elated about his achievement, he realized that raising one peregrine, regardless of how exciting and momentous it might seem, meant very little in terms of the total problem. Unless peregrines could be raised in sufficient numbers, they could never be brought back. Now the most important thing was to breed them with consistency and reliability in order to build up a large captive population. Then, when enough birds could be reintroduced into the environment, some inevitable losses would not cause the whole attempt to fail.

Meng's chief difficulty in the spring of 1971 had been the parents' lack of experience in feeding their newborn young. Apparently adult birds needed experience to become competent parents in much the same way that young peregrines must have actual flying experience to become skillful hunters. In this case, however, too much depended upon the results to allow the parents to gain on-the-job experience as they would in the wild.

Meng decided that the following spring he would take the second clutch of peregrine eggs just before they hatched, place them in an incubator, and after they hatched he would care for

Incubator with peregrine eggs inside. *John Kaufmann*

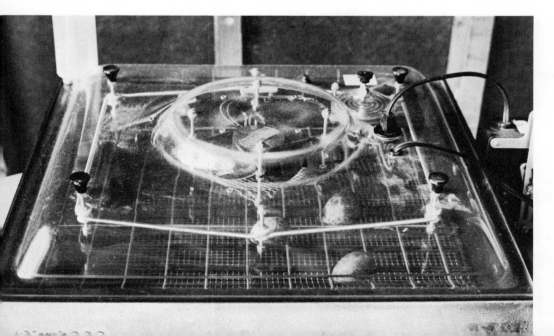

the newborn chicks himself during the first few days, when they were most vulnerable. Then he would put them back on the ledge so the parents could finish raising them. That way, the parents could still gain experience without losing their young. Earlier, he had obtained an incubator that controlled temperature and humidity, turned the eggs automatically every hour, and circulated fresh air inside. Humidity control is especially important during incubation, since water vapor passing into the eggshell prevents dehydration of the liquid contents and keeps the shell wall flexible. In the wild this condition can be crucial when an eyrie is situated so the hot sun shines directly on the scrape for a number of hours each day. When the parent birds return to brood after their daily bath, moisture is passed to the eggs from their damp under feathers.

Meng also worked to solve another problem. In previous breeding seasons he had been unable to see what was occurring on the nest ledge without entering the breeding chamber, climbing up, and disturbing the birds. If he had been able to observe the nesting activities when the parents failed to feed their young, he could have saved at least two chicks. To eliminate this difficulty, he now cut an opening in the hawk house and installed a piece of one-way glass so he could look through at the nesting ledge from outside the breeding chamber without the birds seeing him.

On February 27, 1972, Meng heard the Peale's peregrines calling from the breeding chamber. He looked in through the one-way glass. Both birds were sitting side by side making soft chipping sounds. On March 13, the female was sitting on the nesting ledge when Meng brought food. She came down off the ledge to feed, and Meng went back to look through the glass. Two eggs lay on the sandy ledge. By March 25, when there were four eggs, Meng was sure the clutch was complete. He candled

Female Peale's peregrine defending her nesting ledge.   *Heinz Meng*

the eggs, but they all looked infertile except one, which showed a faint moving shadow as he turned it in front of the light. He put the eggs in the incubator.

On March 28, when most of the eggs had been incubated at least eleven days, Meng candled them again. Two eggs showed nothing, but the other two showed a little shadow, which he thought might be a bubble next to the airspace. Believing that this clutch was infertile like the first one the year before, Meng carefully cut a small hole in one egg near where he had seen the "bubble." To his horror, he could now see the thin, dark lines of blood vessels and the small head of a growing embryo. Realizing that all four eggs must be fertile, he quickly cut a piece of chicken eggshell and fitted it over the hole, sealed it with melted wax and put the eggs back in the incubator.

From this experience Meng learned that an egg should be candled by turning it slowly and carefully in front of the light until it faces in just the proper direction. Then if the egg is wiggled, the darker shape of the suspended "bubble," or embryo, will move back and forth, making it easier to see. If the egg is not turned to just the right angle, the embryo will be invisible, as it was in the egg Meng opened.

Despite his mistake, Meng was pleased and excited that the parents had produced a successful first clutch. Now he waited for the eggs to incubate and for the parent birds to recycle. When he candled the eggs again, he saw that the one he had opened now appeared all dark. However, the other three showed developing embryos. On April 13, he candled one of the good eggs and saw clearly the outline of the head, body, legs, and wings of a growing chick.

Since the first clutch was laid starting on March 11, Meng estimated that hatching should take place at the latest in about forty days, or April 20. On April 16, the first egg was pipped, a small hole appearing in the shell. The chick pips the eggshell by striking outward with its sharp egg tooth. The shell, whose crystalline structure resists considerable pressures from the outside, punctures more easily from the inside out. Nevertheless, it takes a lot of effort for the chick to break the shell. Once the egg is pipped, the chick rests before completing the task of hatching. However, during this resting period Meng could still hear some pipping going on inside by holding the egg up to his ear. He could also hear the chicks peeping inside the shells even before pipping began.

Because of the thin, porous structure of the eggshell, there is considerable communication between the parent bird outside and the chick inside. An incubating parent can hear the chick peeping and pipping, while the chick can hear and learn the parent's calls, feel the warmth from the parent's body, and the turning of the egg. It can also sense whether it is day or night by the intensity of the light passing through the translucent shell.

Once the eggs started to pip, Meng stopped the turning action of the incubator. He could hear peeps coming from the eggs.

Listening to a peregrine egg for sounds of pipping.
John Kaufmann

When he held each egg up to his ear, he could hear the chick working inside to break through the shell. The first one hatched at 1:05 p.m. on April 18. It weighed thirty-two grams. That evening, when its down was dry, Meng took the chick out of the incubator and put it into a brooding box he had arranged. It had a partition consisting of a towel stretched across the box and a heat source, a twenty-five-watt bulb behind the towel. The chick could regulate the amount of heat it received by simply moving closer to or farther away from the bulb. By April 20, all three eggs had hatched.

Meng marked the first chick's wing with red watercolor paint, left the second chick's wing uncolored, and painted blue on the third one, so he could tell them apart. He nicknamed them Red, White, and Blue. By April 25, Meng could see that Red, a female, and Blue, a large male, were growing very well. However, White, a male, was about one-third smaller than Blue and was not doing well at all. He did not eat properly. His toes were shriveled up, so he must have been genetically defective at birth. On May 2, after thirteen days, White died, weighing only 106 grams to his brother's 370 grams and his sister's 522 grams.

On May 7, when Red, now named Princess Anne, was nineteen days old, and Blue, named Prince Charles, was seventeen days, Meng kept track of how much they ate. Princess Anne ate fifteen chicks and Prince Charles ate eleven chicks on that one day. At this age the growing young eat more than their parents,

Feeding the two peregrines hatched and raised from the first clutch, 1972. Prince Charles (left), seventeen days old, and Princess Anne, nineteen days old. *Heinz Meng*

Prince Charles (left), thirty-one days old, and Princess Anne, thirty-three days old. *Heinz Meng*

who must work very hard to keep up with three or four raven-
ous appetites in the eyrie. This observation helps to explain the
phenomenal growth rate of young peregrines, from about one
ounce at hatching to about two pounds, for larger females, in
just thirty days.

On April 10, just sixteen days after taking the first clutch,
Meng found the first egg of the second clutch. On May 14, just
before the second clutch was due to start hatching, he warmed
four brown spotted pullet eggs overnight in the incubator. The
next morning, wearing a padded hat, his heavy jacket, and carrying some pigeon meat in his leather glove, he climbed up the
ladder to the nesting ledge. Both birds screamed at him. The
female jumped off the eggs and grabbed his glove hard with her
beak. Meng quickly took the four warm pullet eggs from his
jacket pocket and laid them on the ledge right next to the peregrine clutch, which he was amazed to see consisted of five eggs!
He put the peregrine eggs in his pocket, pushed the warm pullet
eggs into the sandy scrape, and descended the ladder with the
parents still screaming at him. After putting the eggs in the in-

108

Above, top: Peregrine about to hatch from the second clutch of eggs, 1972.
Heinz Meng

Below: The second clutch, 1972, with three young just hatched and two eggs showing pipping cracks. All five eggs hatched and all five young were raised.
Heinz Meng

cubator, he went out again to check the parent birds. The female was sitting on the pullet eggs and incubating as if nothing had happened. The exchange had been successful.

All five eggs of the second clutch hatched. Meng thus had the unprecedented opportunity to study the process of hatching in a whole series of eggs. He found that hatching normally occurs about fifty-seven hours after pipping. However, if night comes shortly before hatching is to take place, the chick within delays its final effort, sleeping for up to ten hours before finishing its labors early the next morning. In the wild, this delay probably prevents the newborn chick from being exposed to low temperatures at night and also allows it to emerge by daylight when its parents can start feeding it promptly.

By now Meng was ready to give a young peregrine back to its parents and let them raise it. He had substituted the pullet eggs to keep the parents in their breeding cycle and in ready condition to accept a chick. On May 24, wearing his hat, jacket, and glove and carrying some pigeon meat, Meng climbed up to the ledge. In his other hand he held chick number three from the second clutch, now a vigorous, hungry four-day-old, and he also carried a broken eggshell.

The parents screamed. The female grabbed at his glove. The male flew right at his head and knocked his hat off onto the ledge. Meng quickly clamped his hat back on, tossed the pigeon meat on the ledge, snatched three of the four pullet eggs, then placed the little peregrine and the broken eggshell next to the remaining egg.

Retreating back down the ladder, Meng went into the hawk house to look through the glass. The little one was peeping and the female was already trying to brood it. She held the broken eggshell in her beak, then laid it down. Five minutes later she was brooding her "newborn" chick. Later, when Meng could not tell if the parents were feeding the chick, he climbed up again to check. As soon as his hat appeared above the ledge, the male dashed out and seized it, carried it across the breeding chamber, and dropped it on the floor. Meng got it on again and climbed up to examine the chick's crop. It was about three-quarters full. The parents had been doing a good job feeding as well as protecting their young one.

110

Male and female Peale's peregrines with a ten-day-old chick just visible to the left.   *Heinz Meng*

With the chick on the ledge, Meng was able to observe some of the family life of peregrines, although modified by the captive situation. The male rarely did any feeding of the young. He did carry his own food to the upper perch to eat. The female carried food to the young, as she does in the wild, and did most of the feeding. When she left the chick to get food, it would make raspy screams. When she returned and fed it, the chick made soft peeping sounds. Sometimes Meng could hear her breaking off small pieces of pigeon ribs or breastbone to feed her chick.

On June 7, Meng put another young peregrine, number two from the second clutch, nineteen days old, on the ledge. At first this one cowered and hissed in fear, since he had never seen an adult falcon before. But soon he was eating right along with his brother. By now the parents had had considerable experience in feeding. Soon all five young peregrines were thriving along with Prince Philip, Princess Anne, and Prince Charles.

The rearing of all five young from the second clutch was as important an achievement for Meng as his raising of Prince

111

Peregrine Palace, Cornell University Laboratory of Ornithology, Ithaca, New York.   *James Weaver*

Philip. The consistency and reliability of his breeding of peregrines in captivity implied that success could definitely be expected from larger projects in the future. Since the breeding birds seemed to improve as they gained experience as parents, better results could be hoped for with a minimum of human interference. Meng's Peale's peregrines, for example, were now ready to follow through the whole breeding cycle without any egg substitution or artificial incubation, since they had learned to feed and care for their young.

The next step was to start breeding peregrines on a large scale. In 1970, Cornell University's Laboratory of Ornithology built its hawk barn to study the captive breeding of various birds of prey. Since its opening, however, the building has been given over more and more to breeding peregrines, so that it has been nicknamed Peregrine Palace. The large, two-story structure can house up to thirty-eight breeding pairs. It was basically designed after the much smaller forerunner built in New Paltz by Heinz Meng. There are high nesting ledges covered with gravel, and

112

one-way glass panels allow observers to follow carefully the breeding activities of the peregrines. The project is under the overall direction of Dr. Tom Cade, like Meng a falconer and also one of the foremost experts on peregrines.

Falconers from all over the world donated peregrines to the Cornell Project. However, most of them were passage birds like Meng's 1964 pair, and they failed to breed. After his successes in 1971 and 1972, Meng transferred his Peale's peregrines and 1964 passage birds to Tom Cade at Cornell, to be used in further breeding. In 1973, under the management of two expert Cornell falconers, Phyllis Dague and James Weaver, the Peale's peregrines produced seven young. In addition, two other pairs of Cornell peregrines, also originally taken as eyesses, produced thirteen young for a grand total of twenty.

In 1974, an additional twenty-three peregrines were raised at Cornell, a total lower than hoped for due to a fungus in the parents' bath water, which apparently penetrated some of the eggshells and a number of embryos died. However, the production of young was still above that of 1973, and hopefully the fungus infection can be prevented in the future.

Phyllis Dague with a ten-day-old peregrine, one of twenty raised at Cornell's Peregrine Palace in 1973.   *Cornell Communication Arts*

A peregrine killed by shooting.   *Tom Cade*

In any attempt to restock peregrines, the young birds must be raised with an absolute minimum of direct human contact, especially during feeding. If they were to be cared for and fed by hand, they would become imprinted to their handler and be too tame and unafraid of human beings. Releasing such birds into the wild would result in certain failure. They would not have the hunting skill needed to catch wild prey, and they would not be sufficiently wary of people with guns. This danger is very real; many birds of prey are shot each year in the United States, even though all have been given full legal protection by the state and Federal governments.

After they are raised, the young birds cannot be left on a cliff or high building in a favorable habitat to hunt wild prey. They would starve, because even when they have the example of their parents to follow, young peregrines need about a month's to six weeks' practice before they can fly and hunt well enough to feed themselves. In the wild their parents supply food during this time. In captivity their handlers must provide it. Freshly killed

114

prey—pigeons, quail, or chickens—must be left at their "eyrie" twice a day, so that when they fail to make a kill they can return to find food. This procedure, of course, comes from hacking, the old method used by falconers to keep captive eyesses as wild as possible.

In 1974, two Cornell peregrine chicks were selected to act as experimental pioneers for the proposed larger attempts to re-stock peregrines. On June 24, Tom Cade transferred three chicks to Heinz Meng's care in New Paltz. Since the chicks were only three weeks old, Meng finished raising them in cardboard boxes in his kitchen, feeding two of them, a male and a female, without their seeing him. The third chick was to be trained for falconry.

Shortly before, Meng had built a substitute eyrie on the roof of the ten-story Faculty Tower Building on the New Paltz campus. The rectangular enclosure, with sides about two feet high, was set between a low parapet in front and a wall in back. The wall, on the southwest side, provided shade during the hottest

The Faculty Tower on the New Paltz campus. *John Kaufmann*

Above, top: The substitute eyrie atop the Faculty Tower.   *John Kaufmann*

Below: Heinz Meng with the third young Cornell peregrine, 1974, in the eyrie where its brother and sister would stay before their release.

John Kaufmann

part of the day. The top was partly covered so the birds could take shelter in bad weather. A wire screen could be rolled across the top opening to confine the young birds as long as necessary and to protect them from owls at night and hawks by day until they could fly.

116

Looking west from the Faculty Tower roof on the New Paltz campus toward the Shawangunk Mountains. The cliff to the far left is Millbrook Mountain, where peregrines last nested in 1957. A second eyrie, on the right at North Trapp Mountain, was last occupied in 1956.   *Heinz Meng*

The location of the eyrie was superb. To the west stood the high rock cliffs of the Shawangunk ridge, the very place where Meng had last watched the peregrines nesting in 1957. The Faculty Tower is the highest structure in New Paltz, and all around it at lower levels the flat roofs of the University buildings provided many possible landing fields for a young peregrine's first attempt at flight.

When the birds were between five and six weeks old, Meng put them in the covered eyrie on the tower roof. He had banded them and fitted a dummy radio transmitter to each bird, so they would get used to wearing it. When he left their food, Meng would peek in to check their feather growth. He knew that their occasional view of him or his handling them now and then would not affect the birds' imprinting, since their association with feeding is the critical factor in whether they come to identify a pere-

117

The third 1974 peregrine transferred from Cornell to New Paltz, shown here flying in falconry. *John Kaufmann*

grine or a man as their parent. In this case, being fed by an unseen hand, they would mature without definite imprinting and come to their wild ways by instinct.

During this time, Meng was training and flying the third young peregrine regularly, so he was able to judge from its development just about when the pair on the roof would be ready to fly. On July 26, when they were about seven weeks old, Meng put active transmitters on both birds and left the eyrie uncovered so they would be free to leave. Given his freedom, the male took off immediately, sailing out from the roof, swooping around, and scattering the campus pigeons. Later the female also took off from the parapet, but flew down weakly to land on a low flat-roofed building. That evening, after Meng and some observers went home, she took off and flapping hard, tried to fly back up to the tower roof. But she could only manage to reach a tenth-floor window ledge, where a campus janitor spotted her that night.

118

Tom Cade (left) and Heinz Meng attaching radio transmitter to Eve's leg before her release. *Aletta Vett*

Since the greater size of the female causes her to develop more slowly, she takes at least three or four days more than the male to reach the same level of readiness for flight. Meng knew this general fact about birds of prey but had overlooked the practical consequences of it in this case. Now he put the female back in the covered eyrie for several more days to make sure that she would be fully ready on the next attempt. And she was. Soon the two young birds were flying together over the campus, making mock passes at one another, and landing on the roofs of the college buildings.

On one such landing, about a week after release, and while cavorting with the female, the male hopped backward and suddenly disappeared. He had fallen into the narrow flue of a tall chimney on the Campus Learning Center Building. Shrieking in alarm, the female stayed right by the flue, as if trying to help him get out. Risking his life, a fireman with a powerful flashlight scaled the high chimney with ropes and peered down into the

Above: Adam and Eve in flight with antenna wires trailing.   *Heinz Meng*

Below: Eve at the eyrie, with pigeon meat provided for her.   *Aletta Vett*

blackened flue, but there was no sight of the male. A wire screen was placed over the flue hole to keep the female from falling in too. After a daylong rescue effort involving many people, including the New Paltz Fire Department and the State Police, the male was finally located by his transmitter signals and retrieved, black with soot but unharmed, from the fireplace under the chimney.

Soon the young peregrine pair, now appropriately and hopefully named Adam and Eve, were making good progress in developing their powers of flight. They ventured farther out from the tower roof and started to stoop at swallows and other birds. At first their attacks were halfhearted, since they were so plump and well-fed that they lacked the driving urge to hunt and kill. However, Meng and Cade had decided that the most important thing at this time was to build up their full flying strength as fast as possible before they began their long, strenuous, and hazardous migration to the south. Before long Adam and Eve were soaring together on sunny days, tiercel and falcon spiraling upward, mounting on thermals higher and higher and disappearing into the clear blue sky above.

Two weeks after they had first been set free, Meng trapped Adam and Eve on the tower roof using a bow net baited with pigeon meat. He removed the transmitters, which had served their initial purpose, and replaced them with large-numbered bands that could be read at a distance through binoculars. This identification would increase the possibility of people observing and reporting on the pair during their travels.

As Meng released the peregrines, chimney swifts raced past, swallows sailed by, and other birds flew about below. But most important, pigeons were flying above the campus and out over the neighboring farms. A favorite prey of peregrines, pigeons today provide some of the best available wild food, because they

Peregrine swooping past her skyscraper eyrie in Montreal, Canada, in the 1940's.   *G. Harper Hall*

are primarily grain eaters and absorb far less pesticide residues than insect-eating birds. For this reason, scientists hope that nesting peregrines can be established on skyscrapers in cities, where pigeons are abundant.

Peregrines and other birds that migrate to Central and South America in winter are still absorbing large doses of pesticides. For example, Greenland peregrine eggs, which had earlier been thought to be fairly free from contamination, were recently found to contain high levels of residues from parents wintering in South America. DDT is used more and more in poorer countries, since it is the cheapest pesticide available. Until less harmful substances for insect control can be produced cheaply, peregrines and other migrant predatory birds will continue to lead a threatened existence.

Three weeks after the first release, Adam and Eve had still not started to chase pigeons, so Meng helped by entering them, as in falconry. On August 10, he plucked the wing feathers from two pigeons so they could not fly off the tower roof. He left them on the parapet, where the peregrines could see them moving

122

about. But Adam and Eve were not yet ready to kill their prey. They didn't touch the live pigeons but continued eating the pigeon pieces Meng left for them.

A week later Meng tried the plucked pigeons again. The first day nothing happened. However, early the next morning, on August 19, Meng found one of the pigeons killed and eaten. Adam's crop was bulging. Eve may also have fed on the kill, but Meng could not be sure. He replaced the killed pigeon. The next two days, August 20 and 21, Meng checked the roof. There was no sign of Adam and Eve. Neither the live pigeons nor the pigeon pieces were touched. The two young peregrines were gone. Meng assumed that they had begun to hunt on their own after the first kill on the roof and were starting to live in the wild.

Adam flying free over the eyrie atop the Faculty Tower. *Aletta Vett*

James Weaver of Cornell placing two captive-bred peregrine chicks in a Colorado eyrie.   *Gerald Craig*

Adam and Eve were the beginning. Would they survive and return to New Paltz in the future to nest on the Faculty Tower or on the Shawangunk cliffs? No one could really say. The odds were against their lasting through their first year under natural adversities, not to mention those caused by man. But the beginning was successful. Two peregrines raised in captivity were released, appeared to be adapting easily and quickly, and had started to fend for themselves.

There was another achievement in 1974. Dr. James Enderson, Gerald Craig, and James Weaver placed two Cornell peregrine chicks in a wild eyrie in Colorado where a peregrine pair had lost two clutches of eggs due to breakage. First Enderson and Craig put two prairie falcon eggs in the peregrines' scrape, and the pair hatched one egg and raised the chick. Finally, when the two captive-bred peregrines became available, they were substituted for the young prairie falcon. The foster parents raised and fledged the two peregrine chicks. This success opens up the possibility of repopulating parts of the peregrine's former nesting range where some parent birds still exist but cannot breed.

124

Many more releases will come. Cornell will have the capability of raising more than 200 peregrines a year, and other people and institutions will join the effort after its initial successes, no matter what happens to Adam and Eve and the other pioneers. There may be considerable losses among the released peregrines. Bird losses are high under the best of conditions. But the future attempts will be persistent and on a large scale, and the gains will far outweigh the losses. The skill and dedication of people like Heinz Meng, Tom Cade, and others are assurance of success.

Someday, despite man's chemicals, guns, and incessant intrusions into the shrinking wilderness, the falcons will return. Again the high cliffs of New Paltz, Taughannock, Holt's Ledge, Mount Tom, and many of the other silent places will ring once more to the sharp, clear call of the peregrines, returned to live among us.

John Kaufmann

BIBLIOGRAPHY

BOOKS

Baker, J. A., *The Peregrine*. New York: Harper & Row, 1967.

Bent, Arthur Cleveland, *Life Histories of North American Birds of Prey*. (Reprint of U.S. National Museum Bulletin 170). New York: Dover Publications, Inc., 1961.

Brown, Leslie, and Amadon, Dean, *Eagles, Hawks and Falcons of the World*. New York: McGraw-Hill Book Co., 1968.

Forbush, Edward Howe, *The Birds of Massachusetts and Other New England States*. Massachusetts Department of Agriculture, Vol. 2, 1927.

Hickey, Joseph J., ed., *Peregrine Falcon Populations, Their History and Decline*. Madison, Wisconsin: University of Wisconsin Press, 1969.

ARTICLES

Allen, A. A., and Knight, H. K., "The Duck Hawks of the Taughannock Gorge." *Bird Lore,* Vol. 15 (1913), pp. 1-8.

Cade, Tom J., "Introductions to Wild Begin." *The Peregrine Fund Newsletter,* No. 2 (September, 1974), pp. 1-3.

———, "Breeding Falcons in Captivity." *Animal Kingdom* (in press).

Kaufmann, John, and Meng, Heinz, "The Falcons of New Paltz." *National Wildlife* (in press).

Laycock, George, "The Falconer's Paradox." *Audubon Magazine,* Vol. 73, No. 5 (September, 1971), pp. 64-71.

Meng, Heinz, "Breeding Peregrine Falcons in Captivity." *Journal of the California Hawking Club,* Vol. 2 (1972), pp. 105-111.

Meng, Heinz, and Kaufmann, John, "Reintroducing Peregrine Falcons to the Wild." *Journal of the California Hawking Club* (in press).

Zimmerman, David R., "Death Comes to the Peregrine Falcon." *The New York Times Magazine,* August 9, 1970.

126

Many more releases will come. Cornell will have the capability of raising more than 200 peregrines a year, and other people and institutions will join the effort after its initial successes, no matter what happens to Adam and Eve and the other pioneers. There may be considerable losses among the released peregrines. Bird losses are high under the best of conditions. But the future attempts will be persistent and on a large scale, and the gains will far outweigh the losses. The skill and dedication of people like Heinz Meng, Tom Cade, and others are assurance of success.

Someday, despite man's chemicals, guns, and incessant intrusions into the shrinking wilderness, the falcons will return. Again the high cliffs of New Paltz, Taughannock, Holt's Ledge, Mount Tom, and many of the other silent places will ring once more to the sharp, clear call of the peregrines, returned to live among us.

John Kaufmann

BIBLIOGRAPHY

BOOKS

Baker, J. A., *The Peregrine.* New York: Harper & Row, 1967.

Bent, Arthur Cleveland, *Life Histories of North American Birds of Prey.* (Reprint of U.S. National Museum Bulletin 170). New York: Dover Publications, Inc., 1961.

Brown, Leslie, and Amadon, Dean, *Eagles, Hawks and Falcons of the World.* New York: McGraw-Hill Book Co., 1968.

Forbush, Edward Howe, *The Birds of Massachusetts and Other New England States.* Massachusetts Department of Agriculture, Vol. 2, 1927.

Hickey, Joseph J., ed., *Peregrine Falcon Populations, Their History and Decline.* Madison, Wisconsin: University of Wisconsin Press, 1969.

ARTICLES

Allen, A. A., and Knight, H. K., "The Duck Hawks of the Taughannock Gorge." *Bird Lore,* Vol. 15 (1913), pp. 1-8.

Cade, Tom J., "Introductions to Wild Begin." *The Peregrine Fund Newsletter,* No. 2 (September, 1974), pp. 1-3.

————, "Breeding Falcons in Captivity." *Animal Kingdom* (in press).

Kaufmann, John, and Meng, Heinz, "The Falcons of New Paltz." *National Wildlife* (in press).

Laycock, George, "The Falconer's Paradox." *Audubon Magazine,* Vol. 73, No. 5 (September, 1971), pp. 64-71.

Meng, Heinz, "Breeding Peregrine Falcons in Captivity." *Journal of the California Hawking Club,* Vol. 2 (1972), pp. 105-111.

Meng, Heinz, and Kaufmann, John, "Reintroducing Peregrine Falcons to the Wild." *Journal of the California Hawking Club* (in press).

Zimmerman, David R., "Death Comes to the Peregrine Falcon." *The New York Times Magazine,* August 9, 1970.

126

Many more releases will come. Cornell will have the capability of raising more than 200 peregrines a year, and other people and institutions will join the effort after its initial successes, no matter what happens to Adam and Eve and the other pioneers. There may be considerable losses among the released peregrines. Bird losses are high under the best of conditions. But the future attempts will be persistent and on a large scale, and the gains will far outweigh the losses. The skill and dedication of people like Heinz Meng, Tom Cade, and others are assurance of success.

Someday, despite man's chemicals, guns, and incessant intrusions into the shrinking wilderness, the falcons will return. Again the high cliffs of New Paltz, Taughannock, Holt's Ledge, Mount Tom, and many of the other silent places will ring once more to the sharp, clear call of the peregrines, returned to live among us.

John Kaufmann

BIBLIOGRAPHY

BOOKS

Baker, J. A., *The Peregrine*. New York: Harper & Row, 1967.
Bent, Arthur Cleveland, *Life Histories of North American Birds of Prey*. (Reprint of U.S. National Museum Bulletin 170). New York: Dover Publications, Inc., 1961.
Brown, Leslie, and Amadon, Dean, *Eagles, Hawks and Falcons of the World*. New York: McGraw-Hill Book Co., 1968.
Forbush, Edward Howe, *The Birds of Massachusetts and Other New England States*. Massachusetts Department of Agriculture, Vol. 2, 1927.
Hickey, Joseph J., ed., *Peregrine Falcon Populations, Their History and Decline*. Madison, Wisconsin: University of Wisconsin Press, 1969.

ARTICLES

Allen, A. A., and Knight, H. K., "The Duck Hawks of the Taughannock Gorge." *Bird Lore,* Vol. 15 (1913), pp. 1-8.
Cade, Tom J., "Introductions to Wild Begin." *The Peregrine Fund Newsletter,* No. 2 (September, 1974), pp. 1-3.
———, "Breeding Falcons in Captivity." *Animal Kingdom* (in press).
Kaufmann, John, and Meng, Heinz, "The Falcons of New Paltz." *National Wildlife* (in press).
Laycock, George, "The Falconer's Paradox." *Audubon Magazine,* Vol. 73, No. 5 (September, 1971), pp. 64-71.
Meng, Heinz, "Breeding Peregrine Falcons in Captivity." *Journal of the California Hawking Club,* Vol. 2 (1972), pp. 105-111.
Meng, Heinz, and Kaufmann, John, "Reintroducing Peregrine Falcons to the Wild." *Journal of the California Hawking Club* (in press).
Zimmerman, David R., "Death Comes to the Peregrine Falcon." *The New York Times Magazine,* August 9, 1970.

126